ICNC **MONOGRAPH** SERIES

SERIES EDITOR: Maciej Bartkowski
CONTACT: mbartkowski@nonviolent-conflict.org
VOLUME EDITORS: Amber French, Julia Constantine
DESIGNED BY: Hailey Grace Steele
CONTACT: icnc@nonviolent-conflict.org

Other volumes in this series:

Civil Resistance Against Coups: A Comparative and Historical Perspective, by Stephen Zunes (2017)

People Power Movements and International Human Rights, by Elizabeth A. Wilson (2017)

Making of Breaking Nonviolent Discipline in Civil Resistance Movements, by Jonathan Pinckney (2016)

The Tibetan Nonviolent Struggle: A Strategic and Historical Analysis, by Tenzin Dorjee (2015)

The Power of Staying Put: Nonviolent Resistance Against Armed Groups in Colombia, by Juan Masullo (2015)

Published by ICNC Press
International Center on Nonviolent Conflict
1775 Pennsylvania Ave. NW. Ste. 1200
Washington, D.C. 20006 USA

© 2018 International Center on Nonviolent Conflict, Dr. Jonathan Pinckney
All rights reserved.
ISBN: 978-1-943271-16-0 (Print version)
ISBN: 978-1-943271-15-3 (Online version)

Cover Photos: (l) On Oct. 31, 1991, Zambians elected a new president and 150-member National Assembly in the nation's first multiparty elections since 1968. Source: The Carter Center and Northwestern University Library public records. (r) Wikimedia Commons. *Diretas Ja* demonstration in the Chamber of Deputies, Brasilia, Brazil, April 1984.

Peer Review: This ICNC monograph underwent two blind peer reviews that recommended the study for publication with some revisions. After satisfactory updates ICNC released it for publication. Scholarly experts in the field of civil resistance and related disciplines, as well as practitioners of nonviolent action, serve as independent reviewers of ICNC monograph manuscripts.

Publication Disclaimer: The designations used and material presented in this publication do not indicate the expression of any opinion whatsoever on the part of ICNC. The author holds responsibility for the selection and presentation of facts contained in this work, as well as for any and all opinions expressed therein, which are not necessarily those of ICNC and do not commit the organization in any way.

When Civil Resistance Succeeds

BUILDING DEMOCRACY AFTER POPULAR NONVIOLENT UPRISINGS

Securing the ballot box during the Zambian general elections in October 1991. Source: Africa Plus blog (archive)

Executive Summary

Why do some nonviolent revolutions lead to successful democratization while others fail to consolidate democratic change? And what can activists do to push toward a victory over dictatorship that results in long-term political freedom?

Several studies show that nonviolent revolutions are generally a more positive force for democratization than violent revolutions and top-down political transitions. However, many nonviolent revolutions, such as the Arab Spring revolution in Egypt, do not seem to fit this pattern. This study takes on this puzzle and reveals that the answer lies in large part in the actions of civil society prior to and during transition. Democracy is most likely when activists can keep their social bases mobilized for positive political change while directing that mobilization toward building new political institutions.

The study first lays out what we already know about the connections between nonviolent resistance and democratization. It then presents new statistical evidence that nonviolent resistance has a positive effect on democratization independently of other conditions. Additionally, in-depth case studies of Nepal, Zambia, and Brazil—woven throughout this monograph—demonstrate that the positive effect of civil resistance on democratic transition requires continued civic mobilization and a move away from radical, all-or-nothing struggles toward more regular, institutionalized politics. The study concludes with concrete takeaways on how to achieve these changes, designed for civil resistance thinkers, activists, and external actors interested in supporting nonviolent movements.

Table of Contents

Executive Summary 5
Introduction 9
Part 1: What We Know about Nonviolent Resistance and Democratization 12
   Defining Terms 12
      Nonviolent Resistance 12
      Democracy and Democratization 13
      Transitions 15
   What We Know 16
      Nonviolent Resistance Appears to Make Transitions to Democracy More Likely 16
      Nonviolent Resistance has More Positive Effects than Violent Resistance 17
      Nonviolent Resistance Leads to Stronger and Deeper Democracies 18
   What We Still Don't Know 20
      How Strong Really is the Connection Between Nonviolent Resistance and Democratization? 20
      When Does Nonviolent Resistance Lead to Democracy and When Does It Not? 21
   Conclusion 22
Part 2: Nonviolent Resistance and Democratic Transitions 23
   Theorizing the Challenges of Civil Resistance Transitions 23
   Research Methods 26
      Statistical Analysis 26
      Measuring Transitions 29
      Qualitative Analysis: Three Case Studies 31
   Evidence from the Civil Resistance Transitions Data 32
   Evidence from the Brazilian Democratic Transition 41
   Conclusion 43
Part 3: Maintaining Civic Mobilization 44
   Fostering Independent Civic Forces 47
   Holding Victorious Pro-Democracy Leaders Accountable 51
   Maintaining a Democratic Vision of the Future 54
   Conclusion 57

Part 4: Avoiding Street Radicalism 58
    Avoid Extreme Protest Tactics that May Backfire 63
    Support Institutional Channels of Politics 64
    Don't Shut Everyone from the Old Regime Out 68
    Conclusion 70

Part 5: Final Takeaways on Civil Resistance and Democratization 72
    Takeaways for Scholars 73
    Takeaways for Civil Resistance Practitioners 74
    Takeaways for External Actors 75

Bibliography 77

Methodological Appendix 83
    Quantitative Research 83
        Civil Resistance Transitions 83
        Democracy Source and Coding 87
        Civic Mobilization and Street Radicalism 87
        Control Variables 90
    Detailed Statistical Results 93
    Qualitative Research 95

Endnotes 100

Acknowledgements 103

List of Tables and Figures

Table 1.1	11
Figure 2.1	27
Figure 2.2	30
Table 2.1	31
Figure 2.3	33
Figure 2.4	34
Figure 2.5	36
Figure 2.6	38
Figure 2.7	40
Figure 3.1	46
Table 4.1	59
Figure 4.1	62
Table AP.1	85-87
Table AP.2	88
Table AP.3	90
Table AP.4	91
Table AP.5	92
Table AP.6	93
Table AP.7	94
Table AP.8	95

Introduction

The victory of nonviolent resistance movements is deeply inspiring. Thousands of people take to the streets, joining hands to reject an oppressive past and share a vision for a new and vibrant future. The slogans shouted in these moments speak to the hopefulness of these visions: "Solidarity" in Poland in the 1980s, a "New Nepal" along the Kathmandu Ring Road in 2006, or "Freedom, Bread, Social Justice" in the streets of Cairo in 2011, to name a few.

The faces of the people of Egypt the day that President Hosni Mubarak stepped down spoke to the power of this moment of hope. People proclaimed that the country could never be the same—that inevitably they were now on a path toward prosperity, freedom, and new democratic institutions.

The failure of this hope to become a reality has led many international observers to become skeptical, and activists to fear that nonviolently overthrowing oppressive governments may only, in the end, lead to worse outcomes. For instance, during the 2014 protests in Hong Kong known as the "Umbrella Revolution", political scientist Eric Li argued that the protests should be called off because changing political systems through street protests would lead to "Maidancracy", an indefinite cycle of political instability and violent repression (Li 2014).

Autocratic regimes around the world have encouraged this fear, spreading the idea that even the nonviolent overthrow of a regime leads to political instability and violence. Russian President Vladimir Putin is perhaps the most prominent of these voices, decrying the primarily nonviolent "color revolutions" in several post-Soviet states as "tragic" and "irresponsible experiments" (RT 2017), and taking extensive measures to prevent similar mobilizations in Russia and its allies (Finkel and Brudny 2012).

Further, many scholars argue that in the last few years the global political system has entered an age of democratic backsliding. Well-respected data sources on the quality of democracy around the world such as the Polity Index (Marshall 2015) and Freedom House (Abramowitz 2018) have reported consistent democratic declines. Scholars have wondered if new authoritarian norms have begun to replace democratic norms in the international system.

The academic literature on democratization has little to offer activists interested in democratizing their country's political system. Some of the most highly respected scholarship focuses on factors such as a country's level of economic development, geographic size, and religious makeup (Lipset 1959, Teorell 2010)—all factors beyond individual activists' control. Others propose theories of democratization based on specific cases without much wider applicability (O'Donnell and Schmitter 1986).

In particular, scholars have paid little attention to the specific challenges faced during political transitions initiated by nonviolent resistance. Most theories either ignore the means by which a political transition begins, or they focus on transitions that formal powerholders initiated from the top down (O'Donnell and Schmitter 1986). This is surprising, considering that a close examination of the historical record reveals that nonviolent resistance—and, with that, the agency of ordinary people—has played a crucial role in dozens of major political transitions over the last several decades. Some examples are the anti-colonial struggles of the 1960s, the struggles against military rule in Latin America in the 1980s, the anti-Communist movements of 1989-1991, the color revolutions of the early 2000s, and the Arab Spring movements of 2010-12.

This monograph seeks to address that gap by building on existing scholarship and presenting new findings on the transition from a nonviolent revolution to a sustainable democracy. The pages that follow present several "lessons learned" on the need for movements to maintain popular civic mobilization—without letting counter-productive "street radicalism" (defined in more detail in subsequent chapters) take over. Table 1 summarizes these lessons.

Table 1.1: Lessons for Fostering Democracy in Civil Resistance Transitions

MAINTAIN CIVIC MOBILIZATION	MITIGATE STREET RADICALISM
Foster Independent, Indigenous Sources of Pressure	Avoid Extreme Protest Tactics that May Backfire
Be Skeptical of Your Own Leaders	Support Institutional Channels of Politics
Maintain a Democratic Vision of the Future	Don't Shut Everyone from the Old Regime Out

The evidence presented to support these lessons learned includes statistical patterns across dozens of nonviolent transitions from the last 70 years, supplemented by in-depth interviews with activists and political figures who led their countries through some of these transitions.

Chapter 1 focuses on what we already know about nonviolent resistance and democratization, highlighting state-of-the-art research and presenting the gaps that this work aims to fill. Chapter 2 presents theory, research design, and new empirical evidence on the underlying question of whether nonviolent resistance encourages democracy. Chapter 3 presents evidence underscoring the importance of keeping people mobilized during the transitional period and presents three lessons learned on how to facilitate this process. Chapter 4 presents evidence highlighting the importance of avoiding street radicalism, that is, when political transitions derail because the actors involved turn against each other and use the tools of nonviolent resistance to impede new politics from emerging. This chapter also focuses on presenting lessons learned for how to avoid the problem of street radicalism. Chapter 5 summarizes the findings of the study and presents takeaways for scholars, activists, and external actors interested in promoting democracy through nonviolent resistance.

Part 1
What We Know About Nonviolent Resistance and Democratization

How do scholars understand nonviolent resistance and democratization? What does existing work on nonviolent resistance and democratization tell us about how these two phenomena might be connected? And what do we still not know?

This chapter addresses these questions to set the stage for research findings presented in later chapters. First, the chapter defines three key terms: nonviolent resistance, democracy, and transitions. Then the chapter presents three core findings from scholarly literature on this subject, and two areas where our knowledge is still limited.

Defining Terms

Nonviolent Resistance

The scholarly community and popular audiences likely have some notion of what nonviolent resistance is, but those conceptions might be highly divergent. Even nonviolent resistance scholars do not speak with a single voice.[1] A work of empirical scholarship that focuses on nonviolent resistance should begin by clearly describing what this and similar terms (such as civil resistance or nonviolent action) mean. These terms are used interchangeably in this monograph.

Nonviolent resistance occurs when unarmed civilians engage in actions that avoid violence and the threat of violence, targeting political actors such as governments. In this monograph, the term political refers to the broad definition of politics formulated by David Easton: politics as the "authoritative allocation of values" (Easton 1953).

Political struggles are struggles over how communities distribute the things that they value, and the rules that should govern such distribution. Values can be economic, like money and resources, but go well beyond this. Communities value sets of rights and responsibilities for individuals and groups as well, and political struggles often involve disputes over these rights and responsibilities. Seeing nonviolent resistance in the context of political struggle helps us understand a broader spectrum of analytical questions about this subject, as opposed to simply reducing the choice to use nonviolent resistance to a moral or ethical preference.

Nonviolent resistance is first and foremost resistance, meaning it is active political engagement with and opposition to existing authority structures (Sharp 1973, Vinthagen 2015). Actions that lack physical violence and the threat of physical violence do not necessarily constitute nonviolent resistance. Nonviolent resistance as resistance challenges a particular status quo. Political actions that are nonviolent but fall within the normal bounds of regular politics (e.g. elections, lawsuits, lobbying) are not nonviolent resistance.

> *Nonviolent resistance is not synonymous with any one political action, method, or tactic.*

Because of this, context is important in defining nonviolent resistance. The same action may not have the same meaning in different contexts. A march supporting a political candidate in an advanced democracy is not nonviolent resistance, since marches like this are a normal, accepted, and power-reinforcing aspect of such countries' politics. However, the same march undertaken in a country where the political opposition is highly repressed or illegal can be perceived as challenging a political regime and thus is clearly an illustration of nonviolent resistance.

Consequently, nonviolent resistance is not synonymous with any one political action, method, or tactic. In order for an outside observer to know whether nonviolent resistance is occurring requires some degree of familiarity with the power structure in that particular society at that particular moment in time.

Democracy and Democratization

The meaning of democracy is highly contested, understood differently by scholars, activists, and ordinary people. This study examines democracy as it's actually practiced, not a moral or ethical ideal. Democracy may or may not be the best political system. Certain "democratic" systems may or may not be particularly loved by their citizens or admired by outside observers.

The research in this monograph looks at democracy in two ways:

1. A social scientific model that countries can closely approximate but never fully realize, and
2. An either/or perspective based on the presence of particular political institutions.

The first way of looking at democracy comes from the political scientist Robert Dahl, who defines democracy as: "a political system one of the characteristics of which is the quality of being completely or almost completely responsive to all its citizens… considered as political equals" (Dahl 1973, 2). This definition implies that democracies give their citizens unimpaired opportunities to formulate their preferences, signify those preferences, and have those preferences weighted equally (Dahl 1973). Different specific political institutions and practices may move a political system closer or further from this ideal, with democratization defined as anything that leads to movement closer to the ideal.

Democracy in the second sense is informed by the work of economist and political scientist Joseph Schumpeter (1942). Schumpeter proposes a straightforward and easily observable definition of democracy based on political institutions. For Schumpeter, democracy is: "that institutional arrangement for arriving at political decisions in which individuals acquire the power to decide by means of a competitive struggle for the people's vote" (Schumpeter 1942, 241). We may fairly clearly, and with disagreement only over borderline cases, determine whether a country is a democracy. Democracy is an either/or characteristic; it is either fully present or fully absent for any particular political system at any point in time. Democratization is thus the movement from one side of the line to the other and is accomplished wholesale at a single point in time.

Both approaches have strengths and weaknesses. Fortunately, these strengths and weaknesses are complementary. Dahl's view of democracy allows us to meaningfully examine marginal movement closer or further away from democracy but is vague on the boundaries between democracies and non-democracies. Schumpeter's definition is simpler, more straightforward, and helps draw clear categories of what is and is not democracy. However, it does not say much about smaller movements toward greater or lesser democracy. This study uses both conceptions in its empirical analysis and in thinking through the relationship between nonviolent resistance and democracy.

Part 1: What We Know About Nonviolent Resistance and Democratization

Transitions

The final concept to define is political transition. Much of the related research has looked at the ability of civil resistance to initiate political transitions and affect the long-term consequences of a country once a transition is completed.

In their simplest formulation, transitions are the periods between one form of political rule and another. Political scientists typically refer to these forms of political rule as regimes. Any political system, from a small hunter-gatherer band to a large modern state, operates on the basis of a core set of rules, some formal and explicit and some informal and implicit. The most important of these rules have to do with how political decisions are made and how the group that gets to make those decisions is defined (Geddes et al 2014). These rules, when combined, make up the political regime.

Once a regime has been established, it tends to stay in place. Major political players will continue to act based on the rules and routines they are familiar with and avoid disrupting those rules and routines whenever possible. However, certain kinds of shocks can lead regimes to break down. Economic or political incentives within the system may motivate certain actors to try to change the rules to their advantage. Domestic nonviolent or violent resistance or external intervention may also challenge the system.

Because regimes tend to clutch onto power for as long as possible, often these challenges will fail. When they succeed, and the system of rules that was keeping the political regime in power no longer operates, the country enters a period of transition. Transitions are periods where the rules of the political game are unclear—where politics is fundamentally abnormal (O'Donnell and Schmitter 1986).

Political actors struggling during a time of transition will seek to establish a new set of rules that will advance their own interests. A transition ends when this period of struggle is resolved into a consistent pattern of politics, that is to say, when political actors have established a new regime.

Scholars often categorize transitions based on the type of regime that comes into place at the end of the transitional period. Thus, transitions that end with a democratic regime are typically referred to as "democratic transitions", while transitions that go from a prior democratic regime to a non-democratic regime are typically referred to as "democratic breakdowns." Yet it is important to note that transitions need not end with the establishment of democracy (say through a first free and fair election) or an extreme form of dictatorship to be completed. The establishment of any consistent pattern of politics marks the end of a transition. Types of regimes that are between democracy and authoritarianism are not transitional periods if they are in fact consistent, enduring patterns of politics.

What We Know

Having defined these key terms, what can we say about the relationships between nonviolent resistance and transitions? This chapter highlights three key findings and two areas where there is still significant uncertainty.

Nonviolent Resistance Appears to Make Transitions to Democracy More Likely

The first important finding about nonviolent resistance and democratization is that when nonviolent resistance initiates a political transition in a non-democratic regime, democracy becomes much more likely than if other means initiated the transition. In one study, transitions initiated through bottom-up civic movements without violence were more than four times as likely to have high scores on the Freedom House measure of political rights and civic liberties than top-down transitions driven by powerholders (Karatnycky and Ackerman 2005). This analysis broke significant new ground in making the connection between nonviolent resistance and democratization, but the analysis was limited in several ways. It only looked at a small number of cases, used a democracy score of limited applicability (the Freedom House scores), and did not control for other factors that might influence democratization.

Petter Grahl Johnstad (2010) later expanded this work by looking at the effects of nonviolent resistance on other measurements of democracy: the Polity IV database and the Economist Intelligence Unit democracy scores. His work confirmed the connection that Ackerman and Karatnycky had found: Largely nonviolent transitions initiated by civic forces tended to be much more democratic and enjoy higher economic growth than top-down or violent transitions. However, Johnstad also did not control for other potential causes of democratization. This means that we cannot be certain that nonviolent resistance and democracy are not both caused by other factors such as higher economic development or political connections to developed Western democracies. Mauricio Rivera Celestino and Kristian Skrede Gleditsch (2013) addressed this question in a study in the *Journal of Peace Research*. They gathered information on three possible outcomes for every year in every non-democratic country in the world from 1900 until 2004. The outcomes were:

- The country remaining under the same political regime,
- The country changing to a new non-democratic regime, and
- The country changing to a new democratic regime.

They then looked at how likely each of these outcomes was if, in the previous year, a country had experienced a nonviolent resistance campaign, a violent resistance campaign, or no campaign at all. They found that the likelihood of a country changing to a democratic regime was much higher when the country had experienced a nonviolent resistance campaign.[2] Unlike previous studies, they also controlled for some other important potential causes of democracy in their analysis, such as the level of gross domestic product (GDP) per capita, the age of the country's current political regime, and the percentage of a country's neighbors that were democratic. Thus, this study dealt with some of the concerns that the greater likelihood of democracy in countries with nonviolent resistance campaigns could be explained by other factors.

Nonviolent Resistance has More Positive Effects than Violent Resistance

Nonviolent resistance has particularly positive effects for democracy when considered in comparison with violent resistance. While there are some cases of violent resistance movements leading to democratic systems (for instance in Costa Rica after its civil war), overall violent resistance tends to lead to a much more centralized, authoritarian system of control. Nonviolent resistance requires broad social mobilization, and spreads norms of political engagement and activism that can then be used to hold new leaders

accountable. Nonviolent resistance movements tend to have flat organizational structures, and build on dense networks of social interaction, whereas violent movements tend to be less transparent and more hierarchical. These norms and organization structures can then serve as the foundations for new democratic politics.

Erica Chenoweth and Maria Stephan (2011) demonstrated this positive influence of nonviolent resistance in their study on violent and nonviolent resistance movements around the world from 1900 to 2006. They showed that the probability of democracy was almost 10 times higher five years after the end of a successful campaign in countries that experienced nonviolent resistance movements, relative to those that experienced violent resistance.

Similar dynamics are apparent in the wave of both violent and nonviolent resistance movements for independence in the 1950s and 1960s in Africa. Movements that engaged in primarily peaceful urban protest ended up with levels of democracy around 15 to 30% higher than those that primarily used rural insurgency to achieve independence (Garcia-Ponce and Wantchekon 2017). Nonviolent protest created norms of peaceful expression once the countries became independent, and these norms influenced socio-political conduct conducive to long-term sustainable democracy.

Nonviolent Resistance Leads to Stronger and Deeper Democracies

The positive effects of nonviolent resistance go well beyond simply encouraging a basic level of democracy. Nonviolent resistance tends to encourage political regimes that are not only democratic but have greater political participation, have stronger protections for freedom of expression and association, and last longer than regimes brought about through other mechanisms. It spreads norms of political engagement and increases civil society capacity to pressure political elites long after the nonviolent resistance campaign that overthrew the old regime has ended.[3]

For example, in the Polish transition to democracy, the years-long experience of the Solidarity movement that successfully overthrew Poland's Communist government led to a "rebellious civil society" in which protest became a routine part of politics and an effective check on potential abuses of government authority (Ekiert and Kubik 2001). Similarly, Portugal began a transition to democracy following the 1974 "Carnation Revolution," in which hundreds of thousands of Portuguese citizens protested to support a pro-democratic faction of the military. When the revolution succeeded, people spread the norms of public engagement and mobilization, creating local institutions that continued to advocate for democratic change as the transition moved forward (Fernandes 2015).

> *Countries whose democracy was born through nonviolent resistance are much less likely to have democratic backsliding than other regimes.*

A statistical examination of over a hundred transitions from 1945 through 2006 found that nonviolent resistance had a strong positive effect on countries' quality of democracy, primarily along these dimensions observed in cases such as Poland and Portugal: freedom of association and freedom of expression (Bethke and Pinckney 2016). Countries with democratic transitions initiated through nonviolent resistance tended to have much higher formal and informal protections for freedom of speech, freedom of the press, and other kinds of expressive freedoms, and also greater protections for civil society and other political pressure groups independent of the state.

Nonviolent resistance at the beginning of a democratic transition also makes the resulting democratic regime last longer, as measured using survival analysis (Bayer, Bethke and Lambach 2016).[4] Democratic regimes initiated through nonviolent resistance last, on average, around 47 years, while those initiated through violent resistance last only 5 years and those without any resistance last around 9 years. In other words, countries whose democracy was born through nonviolent resistance are much less likely to have democratic backsliding than other regimes.

In brief, many different studies, looking at both nonviolent resistance and democracy in different ways, find a strong positive relationship between the two. Nonviolent resistance appears to be one of the strongest and most consistent factors that lead countries toward greater democracy, whether the resistance consisted of independence movements in Africa, anti-communist struggles in Central Europe, anti-dictatorship campaigns in Latin America, or the color revolutions in the former Soviet Union.

What We Still Don't Know

While the literature on nonviolent resistance and democratization is growing, and the connection between these two concepts is increasingly robust, significant gaps remain in our knowledge about this connection.

How Strong Really is the Connection Between Nonviolent Resistance and Democratization?

While multiple studies have shown a strong relationship between nonviolent resistance and democratization, many scholars still question whether this relationship is real. Most objections revolve around arguments that nonviolent resistance and democracy are part of the same underlying process. When one occurs the other is likely to occur because they have the same underlying causes. For instance, both nonviolent resistance and democratization might be more likely in non-democratic regimes that allow some form of political contestation (Lehoucq 2016), or in countries that have close relationships with liberal Western democracies (Ritter 2014).

Several of the studies referenced above attempt to address these concerns by accounting for the influence of other factors that encourage democracy in their statistical models. But many are limited in the population of transitions that they examine. For instance, Bethke and Pinckney's 2016 study does not examine transitions that ended in dictatorships. Chenoweth and Stephan only look at democratization after violent and nonviolent resistance campaigns, not including transitions where no resistance campaign occurred. Thus, there is a need to continue producing rigorous statistical research that shows the robustness of this relationship across a wider range of different circumstances. This is the first gap in our current understanding of nonviolent resistance and democratization that this monograph seeks to address.

Part 1: What We Know About Nonviolent Resistance and Democratization

When Does Nonviolent Resistance Lead to Democracy and When Does it Not?

Most scholarly work on nonviolent resistance and democratization has compared nonviolent resistance to other kinds of transitions, like those initiated through violence or through top-down liberalization. This has been crucial in showing that nonviolent resistance has a positive effect overall on democratization. However, it means that scholars have not done much work looking within transitions initiated through nonviolent resistance to explain which ones are likely to lead to democracy and which are not.

This is an important question because while nonviolent resistance may have a positive overall effect on countries' level of democracy, on average, there is a lot of variation in whether this positive effect plays out. Nonviolent revolutions have led to strong democracies in places like Chile or the Czech Republic, but they have also led to the creation of new authoritarian regimes in places like Iran in the 1970s or Egypt in the years since the Arab Spring.

Why does this happen? How can we understand the variation in when nonviolent resistance is likely to lead to democracy and when it is not? Scholars have mostly not examined this question. Yet understanding it is crucial both for deepening the scholarly understanding of how nonviolent resistance affects democracy and to generate more effective strategies for activists who are in situations of political transition, where the old regime may be gone but a new, sustainable democracy is not yet fully established.

This monograph seeks to address this gap, first by providing new data that reinforce the strength of the connection between nonviolent resistance and democratization and then by digging into the challenges of what comes after a successful nonviolent resistance campaign through additional statistical testing and in-depth case study analysis. This, in turn, can help us understand better when nonviolent resistance successfully leads to democracy, when it does not, and specific lessons for practitioners of nonviolent resistance to increase their chances of contributing to a successful democratization in their country.

Conclusion

Scholarly research in recent years has yielded significant insight on the relationship between nonviolent resistance and democratization, to the point where we can determine that nonviolent resistance is a powerful way of transforming societies in a more democratic direction. But the relationships between concepts such as nonviolent resistance, democracy, and political transitions are complex, and this means that more work needs to be done. We need to first be sure that the impact of nonviolent resistance on improving the odds of democratization can continue to stand up to scholarly scrutiny. And we need to know why some political systems show the strong relationship between nonviolent resistance and democratization and others do not.

Part 2
Nonviolent Resistance and Democratic Transitions

Theorizing the Challenges of Civil Resistance Transitions

The scholarly literature to date has told us a great deal about the positive effects of nonviolent resistance on democracy. But what can we say about this unresolved question of when nonviolent resistance will be effective in promoting democracy and when it will not? To answer this question, this monograph focuses on the "black box" of the transition period. That is to say, what happens after a nonviolent revolution ousts a dictator but before the new rules of the political game are in place?

Traditionally, scholars of democratic transitions such as O'Donnell and Schmitter (1986) or Przeworski (1991) have modeled the transition to democracy as one in which various political actors have systematic preferences with regard to democratization, as well as various assets at their disposal. Hardliners in the regime strongly reject democratization and instead prefer a strong authoritarian regime. Softliners in the regime prefer a limited opening for democratization. Opposition Moderates prefer limited democratization, and opposition Radicals want transformative democratization. The argument has typically been that transitions are most likely to be successful when an alliance between the Softliners and the Moderates can sideline the extreme demands of both Hardliners and Radicals. If the Radicals push their demands too far then Hardliners are likely to respond with a coup d'état that re-establishes an authoritarian regime.

How does nonviolent resistance at the beginning of the transition change this picture? Two major differences are central: incumbent cohesion and balance of political force.

First, nonviolent resistance has the potential to undermine the cohesion of the previous ruling coalition. Sharp (1973) points to the fragmenting effect that civil resistance has—it provides regime allies with opportunities to defect and join, and even sometimes lead, the opposition. Civil resistance movements can serve either as an alternative community or as a new route to power. Such movement-driven fragmentation of the ruling coalition was key in civil resistance campaigns such as the Rose and Orange Revolutions in post-Communist Georgia and Ukraine (Bunce and Wolchik 2011), as well as in several African pro-democracy movements in the early 1990s (Bratton and Van de Walle 1997, Nepstad 2011, Rakner 2003).

Civil resistance has particular superiority over violent resistance in fragmenting regime control over state coercive forces. Chenoweth and Stephan show that civil resistance campaigns are much more likely than violent resistance campaigns to spark security force defections (2011, 48-50). When civil resistance has successfully demonstrated that the military and other state coercion forces are unreliable, Hardliners second-guess how effective it might be to try to interrupt the transition with a military coup. Their control over the armed forces may be questionable.

Second, in a transition following a nonviolent revolution there is a different form of coercive force available to the groups jockeying for power: new nonviolent resistance. Thus, if, for example, Radicals from the opposition do not find the demands of the revolution suitably met by the new institutionalized politics put in place during the transitional period, they may return to the streets and disrupt the transition.

These basic assumptions frame the contention that civil resistance transitions are unique. They also set the stage for understanding the challenges that are key to moving from the overthrow of authoritarianism to the establishment of democracy.

The first such challenge is continued mobilization of ordinary people during the political transition. Initiating a political transition through nonviolent resistance means that large numbers of people have mobilized to push for political change. Yet keeping these large numbers of people politically engaged in the process of building a new political regime after a successful nonviolent resistance campaign can be extremely difficult. This popular engagement is crucial for keeping decision-makers accountable as a country's new political institutions are being created. If rapid demobilization takes place early in the transition, the balance of force shifts back to the elites, particularly to the remnants of the old regime. These transitions are then likely to lead to limited democratization with a higher possibility of democratic backsliding down the road, for instance, as occurred in Ukraine after the Orange Revolution.

Maintaining high levels of mobilization during a political transition, once the huge task of removing the old regime is complete, is difficult but by no means impossible. Chapter 3 will examine several of the strategies that movements can employ to maintain mobilization and keep their transition on a democratic trajectory.

The second challenge, street radicalism, is in some ways the reverse of the first. Street radicalism disrupts the process of institutionalizing a new political system, which—like the absence of mobilization—can also derail the transition and lead to a fractious regime that falls short of democratic ideals and is ultimately unstable.

To understand this challenge, it is important to remember that almost any nonviolent resistance movement against an authoritarian regime involves achieving unity among widely divergent political and social groups (Pishchikova and Youngs 2016). While these groups may come together for the overall goal of getting rid of a dictator, once the dictator is gone it is inevitable that the different interests and goals of these groups will come to the fore. The unity of the civil resistance campaign will break down.

This breakdown of unity is not, in and of itself, either positive or negative. Politics inevitably involves disagreements. Only in the repressive environment of a dictatorship can these disagreements ever be fully hidden from view. The key questions are: How

Almost any nonviolent resistance movement against an authoritarian regime involves achieving unity among widely divergent political and social groups.

do these disagreements play out in the new political system? Will political disagreements be channeled within the bounds of new political institutions that are being built and consolidated during ongoing transformation? Will ordinary people's equal representation be preserved? And will political competition follow the rule of law? The essence of democracy is that losers in a political contest can accept their losses knowing that the rules of the game will remain consistent and they will have a chance to win in the future.

A successful nonviolent revolution can spread norms and skills related to inclusion and peaceful dispute resolution that can underpin the creation and working of new democratic institutions. Yet it can also provide a powerful set of political tools. In some cases, different resistance actors can use the disruptive potential of these tools to ensure their own narrowly defined interests. This, of course, undermines the creation of regular, broader, and inclusive political institutions and can radicalize politics.

As with the challenge of mobilization, movements can use several strategies and take several cautions to address street radicalism. These will be examined more in depth in Chapter 4.

The above theoretical framing implies three basic arguments that shape the remainder of this monograph, namely:

1. Nonviolent resistance at the beginning of a political transition should make democracy at the end of that transition both more likely and of higher quality. This argument is analyzed later in this chapter.
2. Democracy will be more likely and of better quality when there are high levels of social and political mobilization maintained throughout the political transition. This argument is analyzed in Chapter 3.
3. Democracy will be more likely and of better quality when political competition moves away from street radicalism, even if nonviolent, and is instead channeled through new political institutions. This argument is analyzed in Chapter 4.

Before moving on to these arguments, though, it is necessary to describe the research methods used to examine and test them.

Research Methods

Statistical Analysis

This monograph bases its statistical analysis on the Civil Resistance Transitions (CRT) data project. This project collects data on all political transitions from non-democratic political regimes initiated through nonviolent resistance. The initial list of political transitions came from the Authoritarian Regimes dataset created by Barbara Geddes and her co-authors (Geddes, Wright and Frantz 2014). The original Geddes data include every instance in which a non-democratic regime broke down from 1945 until 2010. The author of this monograph extended the dataset until 2015 and supplemented it by examining each of the regime breakdowns that correlated with the occurrence of a major nonviolent resistance movement, as identified by Chenoweth and Shay in the NAVCO 2.1 dataset (Chenoweth and Shay 2017). The author also identified a few additional cases by drawing on research done in previous work by Pinckney (2014) and Bethke and Pinckney (2016).

The data collection process led to a list of 331 transitions from non-democratic regimes, of which 78 were civil resistance-led transitions. Figure 2.1 below shows all the countries around the world that experienced at least one civil resistance-induced transition during this period (1945-2015). As the map shows, the countries are highly diverse. This is not simply a Latin American story, or an African story, or a European story, but the story of a global phenomenon that has had deeply transformational effects.

Figure 2.1: The Civil Resistance Transitions Map

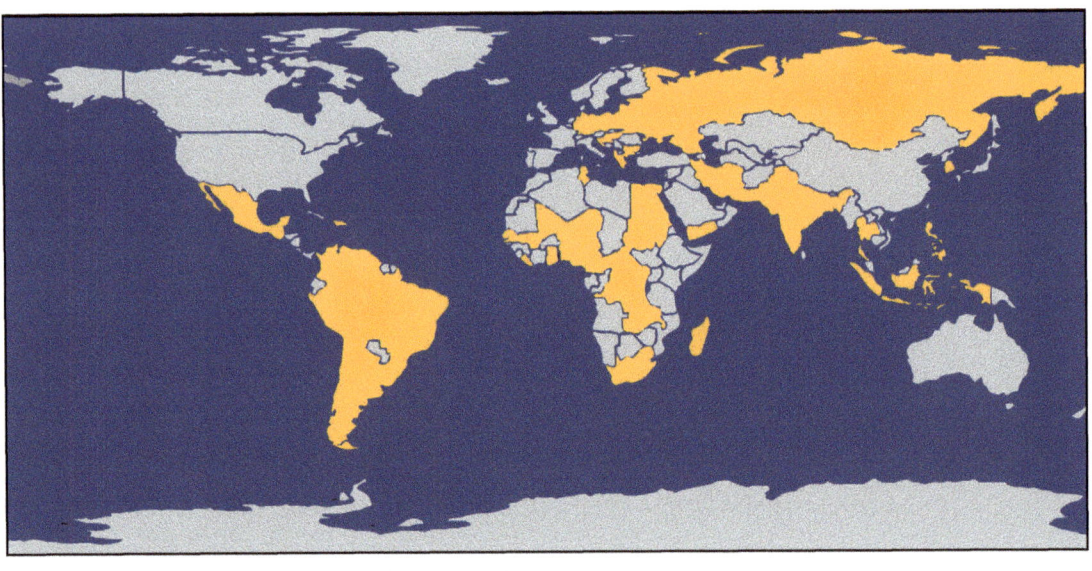

Countries with at least one CR-induced transition from 1945-2015

Source: Civil Resistance Transitions Data (Pinckney, 2017)

Once the cases were identified, numerous other data sources were merged to examine specific questions about the preconditions of these transitions, the dynamics of their transitional processes, and the levels of democracy and types of democratic and non-democratic regimes that followed them. The source for much of this data was the Varieties of Democracy project (V-Dem) (Coppedge, Gerring, et al. 2017). V-Dem is one of the most comprehensive scholarly efforts to track the specific character of political regimes over time. It contains information on hundreds of political indicators, aggregated into several different indexes.

The most important information drawn out of the V-Dem data was each country's level of overall democracy. As discussed above, this monograph measures democracy in both an ideal-type and an either/or way, based on Dahl's definition of democracy as a perfectly representative political system and Schumpeter's threshold definition of democracy as a political system where leaders are selected through a popular vote.

The V-Dem project has as its most central measure of a country's level of democracy the so-called "polyarchy score," which is intended to capture how closely a country approaches Dahl's ideal of a representative political system. It does this by averaging together several indexes along five dimensions that together constitute a representative political system:

- Freedom of expression
- Freedom of association
- The degree to which leaders are elected
- The freedom and fairness of those elections, and
- The proportion of the population that has the right to vote.[5]

The score is measured annually for every country in the world, and ranges from 0 to 1, with 0 being not democratic at all and 1 being fully democratic.[6]

This monograph uses the polyarchy score to test how close a country approaches the ideal-type of democracy. It uses the definition of democracy from the Geddes authoritarian regimes dataset to measure whether a country crosses the democratic threshold, which closely approximates the theoretical definition from Schumpeter described on page 14.[7]

The scholarly literature on democratization is very well developed, with many important arguments about factors that affect a country's likelihood of transitioning to democracy. Thus, the statistical testing in this monograph incorporates several measures to control for three different alternative explanations for how countries democratize: socio-economic modernization, international influence, and past level of democracy.[8]

Measuring Transitions

One major innovation in the CRT data, for its part, is to look at the political transition as a whole as the unit of analysis. Most previous statistical studies on the connection between nonviolent resistance and democratization have looked at country-year data (Celestino and Gleditsch 2013), or measured democracy at an arbitrary point in the future that may or may not represent the end of a country's political transition (Chenoweth and Stephan 2011).

In contrast, the CRT data use the speed of change in political institutions itself to determine the precise endpoints of political transitions, which occur at different points in different countries. In other words, during periods of transition there are rapid changes in the rules of the political game as different groups struggle for power. One reliable way of determining that a transition has ended and that a new political regime is in place is to find the point where those rapid changes no longer occur. When the rules of politics become more constant, we are no longer in transition but rather in a new regime.

Because this monograph aims to explain differences in democracy at the end of political transitions, the type of political change it uses to define the end of a political transition is specifically the country's level of democracy. The analysis measures the level of democracy in each country at the precise point at which this level begins to stabilize, thus allowing us to take into account the particular timing of each country's transition process.

To illustrate, consider the level of democracy in Iran immediately following the Iranian Revolution. In 1979, the Iranian Revolution succeeded in removing the last remnants of the Shah's regime when the revolutionaries ousted Prime Minister Shapour Bakhtiar. Thus in 1979, the old regime had ended. However, a new regime did not immediately come into place after this ouster. Instead, there was a multi-year process of struggle between

Asura demonstration in Freedom Square, Tehran, during the 1979 Iranian revolution. Source: Wikimedia Commons.

various factions as the shape of the new regime was established. Figure 2.2 on page 30 shows that the level of democracy in Iran, as measured by the polyarchy score, did not

Figure 2.2: Polyarchy Levels Around the Iranian Revolution

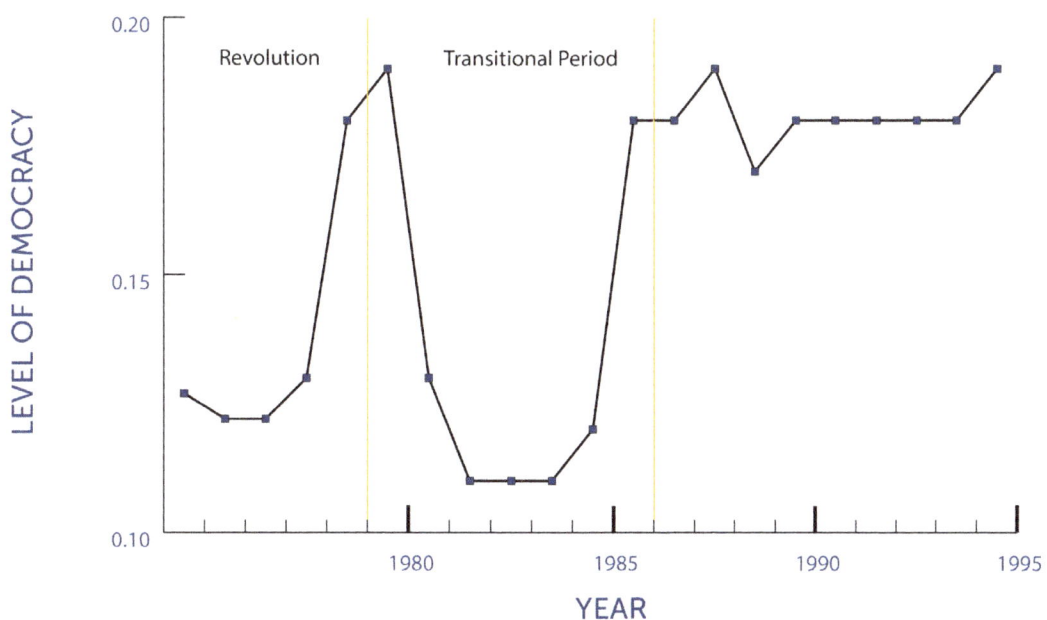

stabilize until 1986. Thus, according to this monograph's system of measurement, the Iranian transition ended in 1986. In evaluating how democratic Iran was at the end of its transition, this monograph measures the level of democracy in the year immediately after the end of the transition (in this case, 1987).

The analysis in this monograph relies on a similar determination for all of the transitions in its dataset. Some have transitions as short as a year in duration and others last as long as 10 years.

Qualitative Analysis

Original field research in three countries that experienced civil resistance-led transitions supplements the statistical analysis. The cases selected were:

- Nepal after the 2006 Second People's Movement, which overthrew the Nepali monarchy;
- Zambia after the 1991 Movement for Multi-Party Democracy, which overthrew the single-party dictatorship of the United National Independence Party (UNIP); and
- Brazil after the 1984-85 *Diretas Já* (Direct Elections Now) movement that led to the ouster of Brazil's military dictatorship.

These three cases were selected primarily for their differences. The goal was to pick cases that shared a transition initiated through nonviolent resistance but that otherwise had radically different contexts. Finding the points of similarity in these otherwise radically different cases could then give leverage on answering questions about the commonalities of transitions that countries with nonviolent revolutions had, despite the fact that they otherwise come from very different contexts. Table 2.1 below lists some of the differences between these cases for illustrative purposes.

Table 2.1: Comparing Nepal, Zambia, and Brazil

	TIME PERIOD	REGION	OLD REGIME
Nepal	2000s	South Asia	Monarchy
Zambia	1990s	Africa	Single-Party
Brazil	1980s	Latin America	Military

In each case, the core of the original research was fieldwork conducted in the country in question. The fieldwork consisted of interviews with key political decision-makers in the civil resistance movement that sparked the transition, and during the transition itself. Interviews were also conducted with journalists, academics, and other close observers of the events surrounding the transition. A total of 128 interviews were conducted over roughly three months of fieldwork.[9] These interviews, as well as intensive study of media and scholarly sources on these transitions, inform the narratives from these cases presented throughout this monograph.[10]

Having defined the key terms of nonviolent resistance, democracy, and democratic transition, laid out the core theoretical positions and arguments, and described briefly the research methods, this monograph now turns to examining its first key argument: *Does nonviolent resistance indeed promote greater democracy in political transitions?*

Evidence from the Civil Resistance Transitions Data

What does the evidence from this new CRT data say? First, it confirms that transitions initiated through nonviolent resistance do, on average, end with much more democratic political regimes than other transitions. Figure 2.3 on page 33 shows this difference. Most transitions not initiated by civil resistance end with a very low level of democracy, around 0.2 on the 0 to 1 polyarchy scale. A 0.2 score is roughly equivalent to Cuba or Egypt in 2016. Very few transitions not facilitated by nonviolent resistance exceed a level that most observers would consider even minimally democratic (a score of roughly 0.6 or more).

While political transitions initiated through nonviolent resistance have much more democratic outcomes, they are not all perfect democracies. Out of the 78 civil resistance transitions, 20 fell short of even the Geddes minimal threshold level of democracy (Geddes et al 2014), with no basic free and fair elections. However, many more exceed this standard than do so in the larger population of transitions not initiated by civil resistance (non-CRTs), which includes violent rebellions and top-down regime change such as coups or elite-led liberalization. Figure 2.4 on page 34 shows this difference in percentage terms. Seventy-four percent of CRTs (58 out of 78 total transitions) end above the democratic threshold.[12] In contrast, only roughly 29% of non-CRTs (74 out of 252 total transitions) end above the democratic threshold.[13]

Figure 2.3: Levels of Democracy at the End of Political Transitions With or Without Civil Resistance[11]

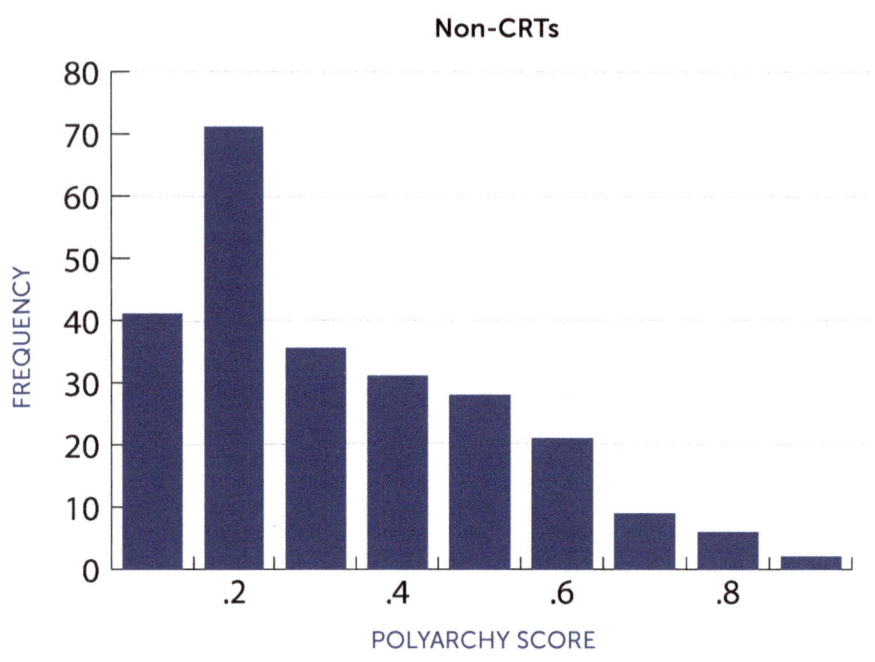

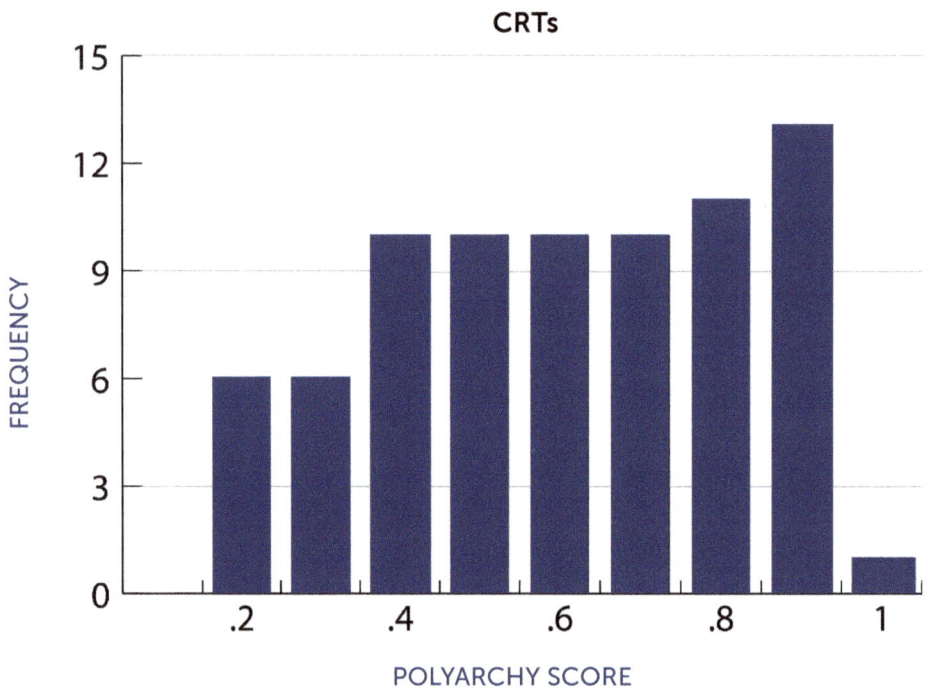

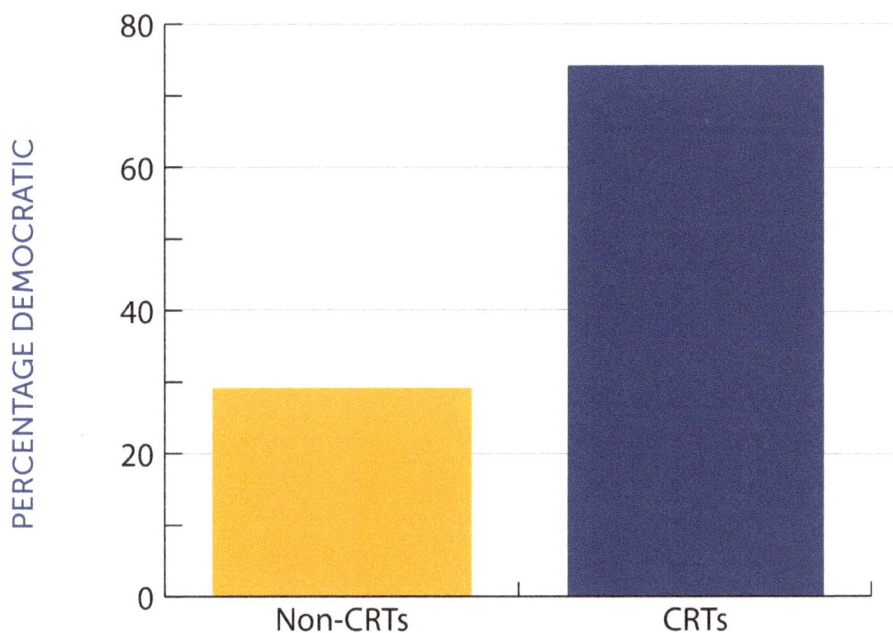

Figure 2.4: Percentage of Democracies at Transitional End Points

One concern commonly expressed by scholars skeptical of the connection between nonviolent resistance and democratization is that underlying favorable conditions can explain the observed correlation between these two phenomena (Lehoucq 2016, Ritter 2014). The same political, social, and economic factors that encourage democratization are also likely to encourage nonviolent resistance. Thus, the argument goes, nonviolent resistance is best understood not as something that independently influences democratization but rather as a frequent feature of a process driven by deeper factors.

Democratization is a complex political process, and it would be naïve to deny the impact context has on its outcome. One cannot assume that nonviolent resistance will be universally effective regardless of the situation. This would be dangerous for the practice of nonviolent action and divorced from scholars' insights. Indeed, the basis for much of the literature on strategic nonviolent conflict is a careful consideration of which tools will be most or least effective after a detailed examination of the power structures that support a political regime (Ackerman and Kruegler 1994, Helvey 2004, Sharp 2005, Mattaini 2013). Context matters, in understanding both whether and when nonviolent resistance will succeed, and whether it will promote democratization.

However, the key point to consider is not whether context matters, but whether it matters to such a degree that nonviolent resistance no longer has any independent impact. This chapter examines three specific questions within the broader topic of whether civil resistance leads to greater democracy:

- Do civil resistance transitions (CRTs) occur in environments more favorable to democracy?
- Does civil resistance still impact democratization when one statistically controls for the most important favorable conditions?
- What is the impact of civil resistance even in situations that are unfavorable?

One obvious favorable condition for nonviolent resistance and democratization is the level of democracy in the pre-transition regime. Democratization is more likely in authoritarian regimes with some limited forms of political competition (Hadenius and Teorell 2007). Similarly, some argue that nonviolent resistance may be more likely to occur in regimes that are not too repressive and allow for some forms of civic engagement (Lehoucq 2016). So, what do the data say? Do CRTs simply take place in authoritarian regimes that are closer to democracy?

The answer is no. The data first show that, regarding their level of democracy, the regimes where non-CRTs and CRTs take place are almost identical. The average polyarchy score for the regimes that come before CRTs and non-CRTs is around 0.23. This is not the worst of the worst authoritarian regimes but reflects a closed and highly authoritarian system of governance. For example, in 2016, countries with scores around this level included Iran (0.23), Egypt (0.22), and Cuba (0.20).

Is this average hiding any differences in distribution of polyarchy scores? This does not appear to be the case either. Figure 2.5 on page 36 shows the distribution of different polyarchy scores in countries prior to political transitions. The figure shows a very similar distribution for both groups, which reconfirms that most transitions—both those involving nonviolent resistance and those that do not—take place in countries with polyarchy scores around 0.2, with a declining number of transitions taking place as the level of democracy gets higher.

Figure 2.5: Pre-Transition Levels of Democracy in CRTs and Non-CRTs

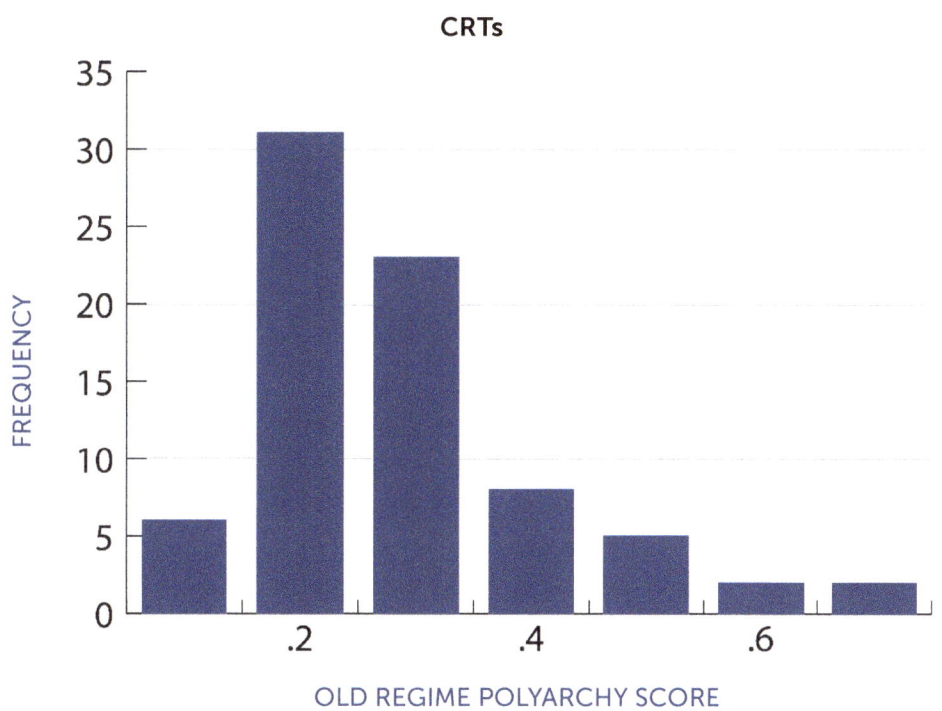

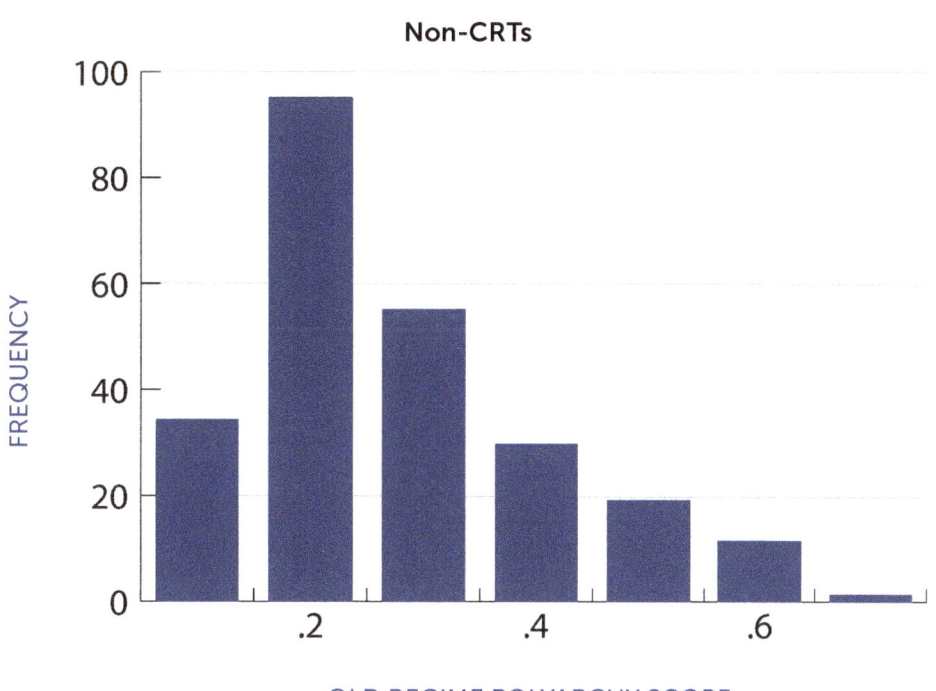

Few transitions of any type take place in regimes with polyarchy scores below 0.1. Thus, as Chenoweth and Stephan (2011) argue, some regimes are just extremely difficult to break down regardless of the methods used (nonviolent or violent), the forces involved (elite or ordinary people-driven), or the direction from which the change was initiated (top-down or bottom-up). The difficulty in bringing down a very oppressive regime is thus not something unique to nonviolent resistance. However, these regimes are few and far between. Out of 288 distinct non-democratic regimes from 1945 through 2015 included in the Civil Resistance Transitions dataset, only 23 had average polyarchy scores below 0.1.

To conclude, civil resistance transitions do not take place in systematically more favorable environments than other kinds of transitions, at least when looking at the degree of democracy in the old regime. We can move now to the second question: Does civil resistance still affect democratization when statistically controlling for favorable factors in the political environment?

A country's prior level of democracy is not the only measure that might explain democracy at the end of a political transition. As discussed in Chapter 1, the scholarly literature on democratization has argued that many factors, such as a country's level of socio-economic development (Lipset 1959), impact the likelihood that a country will transition to democracy. To properly account for these, it is necessary to perform statistical tests that control for the effects of multiple factors that are likely to affect democracy. Thus, this monograph performs statistical tests including all the important controls described earlier in this chapter: socio-economic modernization, connection to the West, the level of democracy in a country's region, and the prior regime's level of democracy.[14]

Graph 1 in Figure 2.6 on page 38 shows the effects of nonviolent resistance at the beginning of a transition on the level of democracy in the year immediately following the end of the transition, when all the other factors predicted to impact democracy are held at their average values. Points A and B represent the predicted levels of democracy in a non-CRT and CRT respectively, while points C and D represent the likelihood of crossing the democratic threshold.[15]

Figure 2.6: Effects of Civil Resistance on Post-Transition Democracy

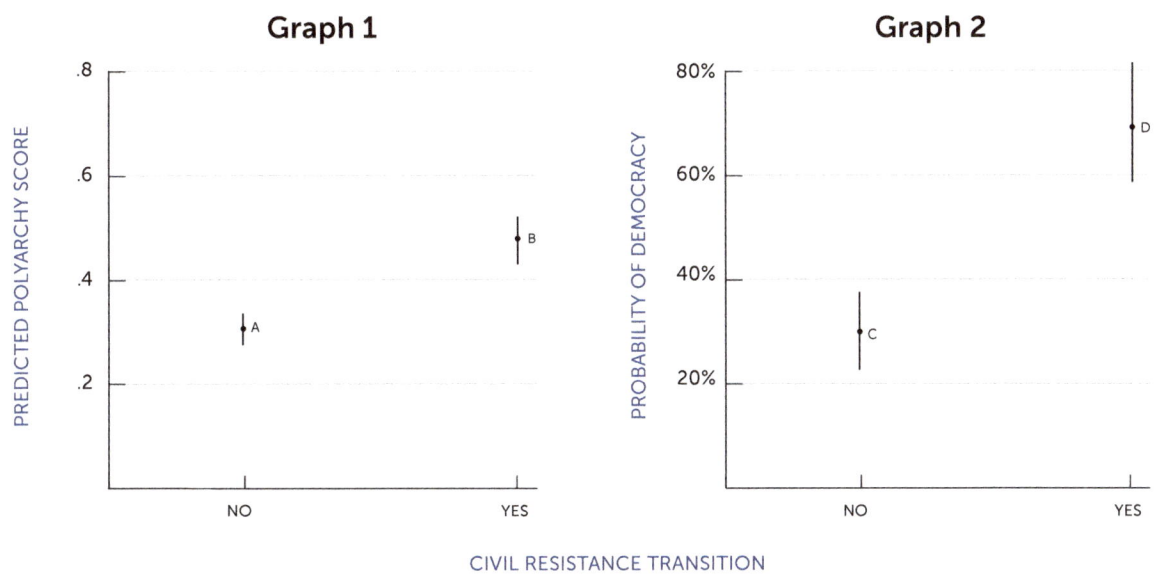

The independent effects of nonviolent resistance on democracy are substantial. Nonviolent resistance at the beginning of the transition increases the predicted level of democracy at the end of the transition by roughly 0.16 on the polyarchy score. For comparison, a difference of 0.16 on the polyarchy score is roughly the difference between the 2016 scores of Venezuela (0.357), a dictatorship brutally cracking down on a nonviolent opposition, and Malawi (0.525), a flawed but relatively stable semi-democratic system. This difference has real-world consequences.

Second, if nonviolent resistance initiates a transition, it more than doubles the likelihood that the country will end its transition with at least some basic minimum level of democracy, as shown in Graph 2. Point C is the probability of democracy at a transition's end without civil resistance, while Point D is the probability of democracy with civil resistance. Without civil resistance, the probability of crossing the democratic threshold at the end of a transition is roughly 30%. With civil resistance, this probability jumps to around 70%.

It is helpful to compare this to the effects of other factors that influence democratization. In this statistical model, to achieve the same increased likelihood of democratization in the absence of any nonviolent resistance, a country's pre-transition level of democracy would have to be at 0.44, very high for a non-democratic regime.[16] In other words, when nonviolent resistance is absent, only countries that are already very close to democracy have even a small chance of democratizing. With nonviolent resistance, even extremely authoritarian countries may democratize.

This discussion leads naturally into the third question: What is the effect of nonviolent resistance even when conditions are highly unfavorable? As the numbers along the vertical axes of the graphs in Figure 2.6 show, holding other factors constant, even if nonviolent resistance increases the predicted level of democracy, high democratic quality is still not guaranteed (see page 38).

At the same time, on average, negative contextual factors such as a highly undemocratic prior regime do suppress the likelihood of democracy even in civil resistance transitions. Yet the data show that CRTs have the potential to achieve high levels of democracy even in unfavorable conditions. Figure 2.7 on page 40 shows this relationship. It compares the percentage of transitions that ended as democracies in CRTs and non-CRTs in countries that, prior to their transitions, were extremely undemocratic, mostly undemocratic, or only slightly undemocratic.[17] Even in the extremely undemocratic countries, over 70% of CRTs ended as democracies. Only around 20% of non-CRTs democratized in either extremely undemocratic or mostly undemocratic countries.[18]

To answer the third question, we may conclude that, while favorable conditions make democratization more likely, even in very unfavorable conditions, initiating a political transition through nonviolent resistance is much more likely to lead to democracy than initiating a transition through violence, top-down liberalization, or external intervention.

Figure 2.7: Pre-Transition Levels of Democracy and Post-Transition Democracy

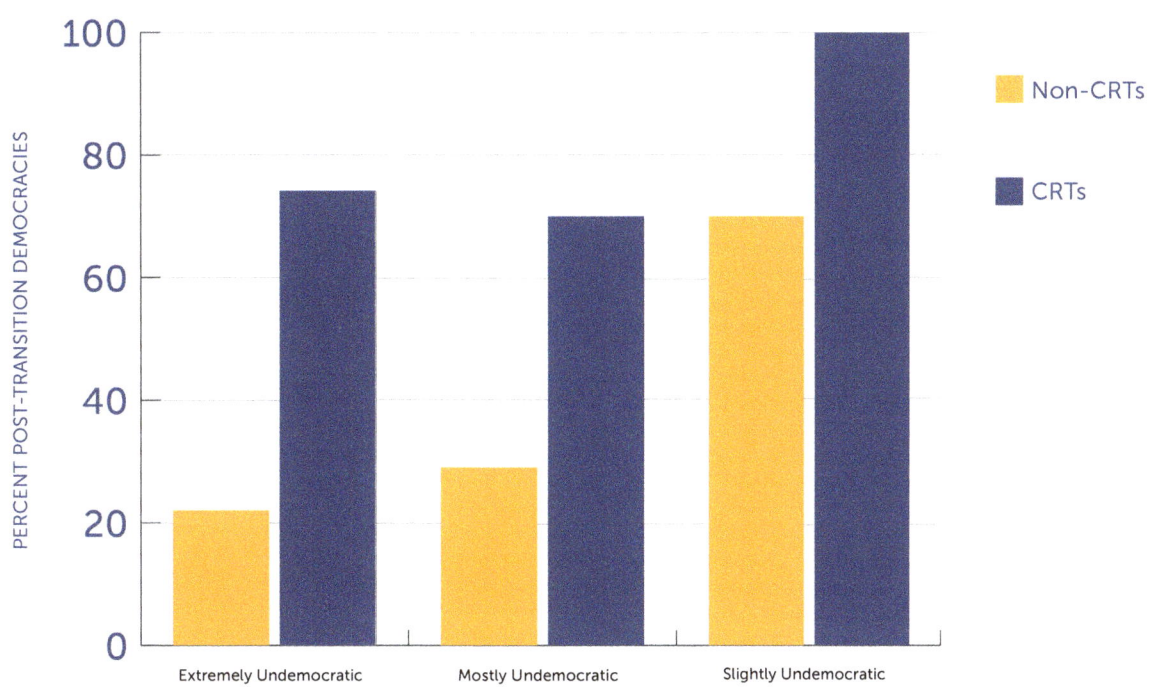

The statistical evidence strongly supports the contention that nonviolent resistance plays a strong democratizing role. This role cannot be explained by favorable conditions. Civil resistance occurs and succeeds in some of the worst and most repressive regimes. It is not a foolproof panacea, and factors like a country's regional political context or level of socio-economic development play an important role in shaping the likelihood of democratization. However, even in extremely undemocratic countries, civil resistance dramatically shapes a country's political transition, leading to a much higher likelihood of democratization.

Evidence from the Brazilian Democratic Transition

Looking at a specific case helps illustrate the positive statistical relationship between nonviolent resistance and democratization described in the previous section. In Brazil, one of the cases this monograph examines in depth, many scholars have argued that democratization was mostly the result of top-down liberalization efforts by progressive members of the military government.

Diretas Já demonstration in the Chamber of Deputies, Brasilia, Brazil, April 1984. Source: Wikimedia Commons

But this picture of Brazil's authoritarian regime leaves out a great deal of crucial grassroots organizing undertaken by the country's broad, diverse opposition. Initially, in the late 1960s and early 1970s, significant portions of the opposition attempted to challenge the Brazilian government through armed resistance. Student groups and radical leftist groups attempted to start several different guerrilla movements to overthrow the military government. However, the Brazilian military and right-wing paramilitary groups were able to quickly and brutally suppress the movement through the superior use of overwhelming violent force (Almeida 2015, Teles 2017).

The military dictatorship's suppression of violent resistance led to a consensus among the opposition that violence would be ineffective in ending authoritarianism in Brazil (Goertzel 1999, 70-72, Kinzo 1988). Thus, by the late 1970s, different segments of the opposition joined together primarily in the broad-based opposition political party, the Brazilian Movement for Democracy (MDB). MDB had embraced a nonviolent strategy of gradually building up institutional power and influence as well as pressuring the regime through more traditional avenues of nonviolent resistance such as protests and strikes.

Beginning with President Ernesto Geisel in 1974, the Brazilian military began scaling back the authoritarian structures of their regime. They relaxed censorship rules and allowed for greater freedom of association. Yet the intention of these measures was not to lead Brazil towards a democratic future. Instead, the measures were intended to further legitimize military rule by allowing for minimal competition among "responsible elites" (Schneider 1991, 269).

However, the country's opposition saw an opportunity in this limited opening to push further toward a full-fledged democratic transition. Many different types of opposition groups pursued this activism, from national level groups, such as the MDB and the labor movement, to local religious and community organizations. Whenever the regime would offer minor concessions, the country's nonviolent resistance movements would quickly latch on to them and popularize demands for increased freedom to pressure the regime not to revoke these concessions. This, in turn, would snowball into new movement demands and further concessions by the regime.

For example, in 1979, the military government passed significant reforms on the creation of political parties, for the first time allowing more than a single opposition party. By all accounts, the intention of this reform was primarily to undermine and divide support for the MDB, ensuring the ability of the government's party to continue to dominate most elections. As part of the law, the government required that all political parties have the word "Party" in their names. This forced the MDB to rename itself, a move the government hoped would undermine their popularity by diluting their brand.

However, the opposition outplayed the regime and used this divide and conquer attempt to improve their political position and push the regime toward greater liberalization. The MDB simply renamed itself the Party of the Brazilian Democratic Movement (Portuguese initials PMDB) and kept much of its support. In addition, other forces from the opposition quickly jumped at the opportunity to create several new political parties that, far from dividing a limited opposition space among competing factions, actually increased popular mobilization and political engagement. Most prominently, the labor movement formed the Worker's Party (PT), which would become a major political force during the transition and in Brazil's new democratic regime.

The nonviolent opposition movement reached its peak in 1984, when opposition crystallized around a single demand: that the Brazilian president, indirectly elected by an electoral college and held by a general since the military coup of 1964, be directly elected by the people. Millions took to the streets across Brazil in the so-called *Diretas Já* ("Direct Elections Now") campaign. The campaign's most immediate demand was that the Brazilian legislature, dominated by loyalists of the military regime, pass a constitutional amendment, proposed by PMDB legislator Dante de Oliveira, to create direct elections for the presidency. While the Brazilian legislature did not pass the amendment, the mobilization sparked mass defections from the ruling party and led the parliament to elect the country's first non-military president since the 1960s.

Furthermore, the country's nonviolent opposition demanded that a new constitution fundamentally transform the country's political system. Popular groups from the country's labor movement, churches, women's movement, and others were involved in large-scale activism which also fed into drafting the new constitution. The result was a constitution that involved some of the most progressive protections in Latin America, including a constitutionally guaranteed right to strike (Martinez-Lara 1996).

Had it not been for nonviolent resistance, the Brazilian transition would have likely taken a turn from military dictatorship to that of an elite semi-democracy dominated by the traditional economic allies of the military. Nonviolent resistance from below forced those in power to open up the political system to minimal competition in order to co-opt potential opposition and maintain a veneer of democratic legitimacy. Further, it compelled the regime to agree to a new democratic system that protected fundamental freedoms and human rights.

Conclusion

Thus, evidence from scholarly literature, statistical analysis, and the presented case of political transitions is clear. Nonviolent resistance is a powerful and consistent democratizing force. Relative to other means of achieving political change, nonviolent actions are the most effective way of ensuring that a country will move from a non-democratic political system to one that is democratic and protects political freedoms.

Having confirmed this finding, we can now move to the issue of why successful civil resistance sometimes fails to lead to democracy. How does democratization happen in these cases? And, if we understand how it happens, why does it sometimes not happen? What lessons can we learn about why nonviolent resistance sometimes leads to democracy and sometimes does not?

Part 3
Maintaining Civic Mobilization

The first set of challenges all arise from one fundamental underlying problem: In many cases, after a civil resistance movement has ousted a dictator, it is difficult to keep people in the streets to continue to push for major changes. Much of the mobilization that drives civil resistance movements to success comes from "negative coalitions"—movements based not on a single shared vision of the future but on distaste for a hated non-democratic government (Beissinger 2013, Tucker 2007).

Why is mobilization important during the transition, once a dictator has been ousted? Because the impact of nonviolent resistance on democratization is indirect. It operates through intermediate steps: bringing new leaders with democratic preferences into positions of power, spreading skills and attitudes of civic engagement, and creating accountability mechanisms for new political leaders and remnants of the old regime. None of these intermediate steps is inevitable. Ensuring them requires sustained mobilization.

One mechanism that may explain the positive effect of nonviolent resistance on democratization is that nonviolent resistance puts in positions of power and influence leaders who are more likely to have pro-democratic values. People who already have these values are more likely to choose to participate in a nonviolent resistance movement. In addition, the experience of participating in a movement itself is likely to foster values of consensus-based, nonviolent decision-making. Still, we must be reminded that in a nonviolent revolution the people who led the movement are not the only major political players. A successful nonviolent revolution is likely to leave many of the people who ruled as part of the old government in positions of potential influence. Some of them may accept the new democratic rules of the political game but others may become spoilers.

Nonviolent resistance puts in positions of power and influence leaders who are more likely to have pro-democratic values.

Even if these figures from the old regime have joined the nonviolent resistance movement during its period of struggle, they may not share particularly democratic preferences. Many may have chosen to withdraw their support not because of fundamental changes in heart, but for more short-term political advantage. As Gene Sharp reminds us, nonviolent resistance rarely works through "conversion," in which nonviolent resistance causes the opponent to share the resister's goals. Instead, its mechanisms of success are more typically "accommodation," and "nonviolent coercion," in which the fundamental underlying views of the opponent are not changed but they give in to the goals of the resister because it is in their interest to do so (Sharp 2005).

Maintaining mobilization during the transitional period is thus crucial to maintaining a degree of public scrutiny and accountability over those who may not have underlying preferences for the goals of the revolution to continue to support it.

A second mechanism that scholars have identified to explain the positive effect of nonviolent resistance on democratization is that the experience of political participation through nonviolent resistance gives ordinary people a set of tools and a feeling of political efficacy that they can then use to push forward democratizing political agendas in the transition (Bethke and Pinckney 2016). Yet for these tools to be passed on from the group of people who participated in the nonviolent resistance movement that ousted the dictator, they must be practiced. If everyone simply goes home when the dictator is gone then these skills and traditions will be unlikely to continue throughout society, and the tradition of resistance will fade.

Statistical analysis of the Civil Resistance Transitions data underscores the importance of transitional mobilization. In a statistical model of the level of democracy at the end of a civil resistance transition, mobilization had a highly statistically significant influence.[19] Figure 3.1 on page 46 shows this relationship.[20] Moving from a very low level of mobilization to a very high level of mobilization led to an increase of almost 0.35 in the level of democracy, controlling for the influence of other major explanations of democracy.[21]

Figure 3.1: Transitional Mobilization in Civil Resistance Transitions[22]

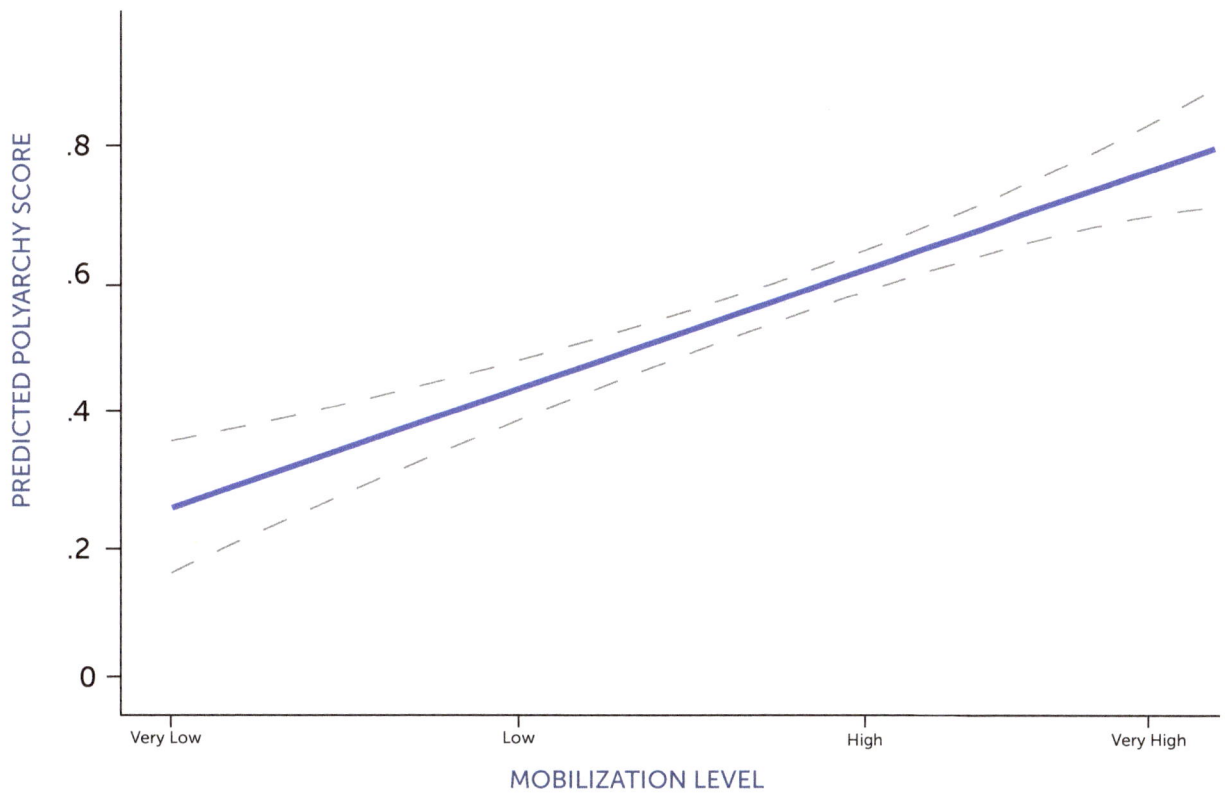

If civic mobilization during a transition is important for leading a country from an autocracy to a sustainable democracy, how can such mobilization be encouraged? What can the historical examples and lessons of transitions teach us about how to make sure that people do not simply go home once the dictator is gone and the transition has begun?

This monograph identifies three key practices that can help maintain healthy civic mobilization:

1. Foster independent civic forces
2. Question and hold new leaders accountable
3. Maintain a positive and democratic vision of the future

Fostering Independent Civic Forces

One key challenge in maintaining mobilization during the transition is establishing or supporting advocacy structures that are independent. This includes structures of new elites who have just come to power—often the leaders of the successful nonviolent resistance movement—as well as structures of outside forces, typically other countries or international NGOs. Perhaps more critical still for democratization are sources of political pressure—namely civic forces that can speak with independence and authority on the important issues of democratization, hold new leaders accountable, and keep pushing the transition in a democratic direction.

The specific shape of these independent forces will differ depending on the political and social dynamics of the country. In some places, religious institutions can serve as an important source of independent pressure. In other places, labor unions have served this function. In still others, it falls to civil society organizations that explicitly carry mandates that encourage democratization, social progress, or economic development. Activists should consider the dynamics of their own societies in determining which existing institutions could serve in this role or might need to be created to fulfill this function.

While differences between countries will be vast, there are a few key characteristics of institutions that activists should look for or look to develop:

- Independence from new political elites and ability to criticize and put pressure on them without being subject to charges of partisan hypocrisy, and
- Deep connection to the needs and interests of ordinary people, and willingness to follow those needs rather than the dictates of external allies or supporters.

Finding or creating organizations that meet the first criterion is difficult in the context of a civil resistance transition because most successful civil resistance campaigns bring together those seeking political power with society's civic institutions. Activists and politicians often march arm in arm during nonviolent struggles. Alliances are common between opposition political parties seeking to gain positions of power on the one hand, and civil society groups motivated to achieve deeper kinds of transformations on the other. This is a good and necessary thing in the context of encouraging the unity needed to bring down a dictatorship through nonviolent resistance. At the same time, it means that once the old regime is gone and those opposition politicians are in positions of power, the lines can be blurred between these new elites and the societal forces that could hold them accountable.

But are these blurred lines a problem? Why can't pressure for democratization come from those who now hold the levers of power? Because political leaders, even in a political system moving toward democracy, face their own professional and personal incentives. And those incentives focus on one key thing: holding onto power. Therefore, it is crucial that the desire to hold onto power be directly connected to how good a political leader is at putting in place democratic reforms that serve the public good. The best way to create this connection is through independent civic groups that can mobilize in favor of these reforms if needed.

Therefore, activists who have put their lives on the line in a nonviolent resistance movement and want to see a democratic system established will need to pressure politicians to follow through on delivering that system. That pressure can best be achieved through forces that are not part of the institutional struggle for political power.

The common phrase used to describe such forces of independent pressure is "civil society." Yet, in much of the developing world, this phrase brings forth an image of formalized and elitist organizations that exist primarily to pursue international funding and, often based in capitals and large urban areas, have little connection to the day-to-day struggles of ordinary people.[23] Effective pressure can certainly come from these kinds of organizations. However, much more frequently, effective independent pressure comes from organizations that are more deeply rooted in their local community.

Independent civic forces should also have a significant degree of independence from international sources of power such as donor countries and foundations. International assistance may play an important role in helping nonviolent resistance movements (though the role is often overstated). However, it can also be harmful to the long-term mobilization potential of a movement.

Why is this so? The reasons are the inherent differences in goals between international donors and local movements. International NGOs are driven not just by altruistic desires to improve peace, development, and democracy but also by materialistic incentives of competition, uncertainty, and insecurity.[24] While there are certainly exceptions, the long-term process of building up independent sources of civic

Part 3: Maintaining Civic Mobilization

power and pressure during a political transition is unlikely to always be in line with these external incentives. If the domestic agenda is dominated by international actors, then it is likely to shift in directions unhelpful to grassroots mobilization.

In some instances, the goals of international donors may even undermine the domestic goal of setting up independent civic entities. Particularly in developing countries—the vast majority of countries that have experienced nonviolent revolutions since 1945—the resources of the international community far outstrip local resources. This means that international priorities may easily crowd out domestic priorities, shifting talented local leaders away from goals and projects more deeply connected to the needs and desires of the people, and toward projects and office-based work tailor-made to secure international funding and implement pet projects driven by donors' priorities.

The best way to keep ordinary people engaged is to have activists and movement leaders stay close to their needs and preferences. Getting too close to new political leaders can blur the lines between advocacy and the struggle for power. Getting too close to international allies can shift priorities away from the needs of the grassroots.

In some instances, the goals of international donors may even undermine the domestic goal of setting up independent civic entities.

The political dynamics in **Nepal** following the 2006 transition illustrate the challenges of civic forces lacking independence from new political elites and international donors. After the 2006 ouster of King Gyanendra, there was a fairly robust level of mobilization still in the country. But this mobilization fell almost exclusively into two camps: competition between the country's political parties, and internationally organized and funded efforts that lacked local buy-in. The results of these patterns of mobilization were so destructive that one activist interviewed for this project questioned whether the country had ever truly had a "movement" at all.

Nepal certainly had its fair share of activists struggling for better governance, human rights, and other positive, democratic goals. But, reflecting a widespread perception, many people interviewed for this project reported that activists in civil society were nothing more than politicians for whom it was currently inconvenient to hold political office. Many interviewees also dismissed civil society activists as self-interested professionals attempting to enrich themselves off of the largesse of international organizations that came to Nepal with their own agendas. The exceptions to this general pattern came from the few sources of political pressure that maintained mobilizational capacity but focused on pressuring those in power around particular issues intimately connected to the needs of local constituencies.

One example was a movement that the Nepali Dalit[25] community led in 2015 to ensure that protections for Dalit rights were included in Nepal's new constitution. During the constitution-drafting process, activists learned that the country's interim parliament intended to remove protections that they had previously promised the Dalit community. Immediately, Dalit leaders held a series of meetings to strategize about how to put pressure on the political parties to get those protections back. After a period of three to four months, during which the Dalit community led a series of political actions, street protests, and lobbying, the political parties added the demanded protections back into the constitution.

Many of the prominent leaders in this movement benefitted from widespread credibility among the Dalit community. These leaders acted independently from political parties competing for control of the Nepali government. For example, it was well known that Padam Sundas of the Samata Foundation turned down political positions that several different parties had offered him. As they did with other leaders like him, the Dalit community perceived Sundas' demands for political protections as genuine and legitimate, and not as a bid to benefit his own political fortune.

The impetus for leaders' actions was also entirely indigenous, based on a lengthy series of discussions within the Dalit community on the rights and protections that they wanted in the new constitution. Because the decision to take action and the specific

Nepal's 2006 Democracy Movement is also referred to as *Jan Andolan* ("People's Movement"), implying that it is a continuation of the 1990 *Jan Andolan*. Source: Wikimedia Commons.

goals of the action had come from within the community, rather than from any external source, there was widespread buy-in from Dalits all across the country. This generated significant participation in street protests and formal political lobbying.

Independence from political parties and from external allies was key in explaining this movement's success. This illustrates the broader importance of focusing mobilization around forces independent from the struggle for political power and from the incentives of international actors.

Holding Victorious Pro-Democracy Leaders Accountable

Highly charismatic leaders are often at the forefront of nonviolent resistance movements. These leaders often undergo tremendous personal sacrifice to achieve freedom for their people. It can be a tempting prospect to hope that, once these people are in power, they will fix the country's major political and social problems simply by approaching politics with an unshakeable moral code and the best interests of the people at heart.

Certainly, one can easily think of exemplary leaders such as Nelson Mandela or Vaclav Havel who, in many ways, lived up to these hopes. However, the sad truth is that civil resistance leaders sometimes find the practices of the old dictators appealing once the levers of political power are under their control. Yet because these leaders have such heroic pasts, people are often hesitant to criticize them. It is difficult to reject a leader who has gone through suffering and sacrifice for the sake of ending oppression. This hesitancy undermines the effectiveness of public accountability and can thus ultimately derail democratic progress.

The case of **Zambia** provides a powerful illustration of the dangers when civil society in transition does not dare to question its new political leaders or questions its new leaders without any particular force behind them. The Movement for Multi-Party Democracy (MMD) mobilized in 1990-1991 to bring down the single-party regime of President Kenneth Kaunda and the United National Independence Party (UNIP). While a large group of prominent figures came together to found the movement, by the time the MMD successfully challenged President Kaunda in Zambia's 1991 presidential election, two major transformations had occurred. First, the MMD had re-shaped itself from a diffuse social movement into a political party and, second, control over that party had become heavily centralized around party presidential candidate Frederick Chiluba.

Chiluba, a charismatic leader in the country's national union (the Zambian Congress of Trade Unions or ZCTU), had been a dissident and critic of the government for many years. In 1980, he spearheaded a national strike campaign to protest government policies that centralized control of local government in the hands of the ruling party. He spoke out against the abuses of the single-party regime when it was unpopular and costly to do so. This activism cost Chiluba dearly, including time in prison for a significant period.

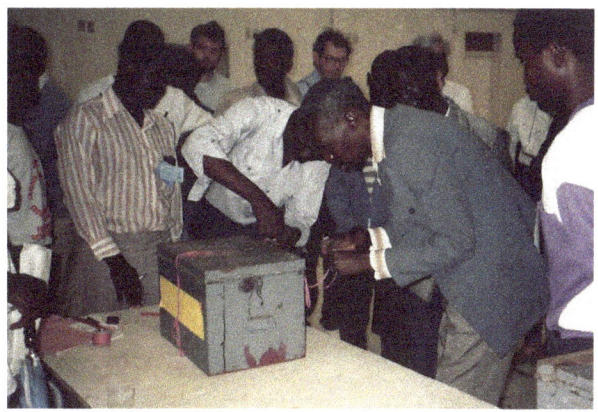

Securing the ballot box during the Zambian general elections in October 1991. Source: Africa Plus blog (archival photo)

His activism, long-time leadership of the ZCTU, and inspiring public speaking led Chiluba to become an extremely popular and admired figure, not just in the MMD inner circles but across the country. Eventually, this helped Chiluba trounce President Kaunda in the 1991 election, winning the presidency with 76% of the vote.

Chiluba maintained his popularity throughout his time in office, allowing him to implement a number of very unpopular economic liberalization measures demanded by international institutions that wound down the quasi-socialist institutions of the old single-party state. Some Zambian political elites interviewed for this monograph saw this as a positive thing. The president's popularity allowed him to make some bold and difficult policy changes that would have been almost impossible for a less popular administration.

However, there was a significant negative side to Chiluba's popular support and its pernicious effects have continued until today. Soon after entering office, President Chiluba made a statement that almost all the Zambians interviewed for this project[26] remembered and saw as prescient for his later behavior: that before becoming president he "never knew that power could be so sweet." While different sources contest the details, in broad strokes it is very clear, and was reported by almost all interviewees for this study, that Chiluba's administration very quickly became mired in political corruption. Finally having the reins of power in his hands, President Chiluba did not stay true to the democratic ideals that he had ridden into office but instead began using the state for his own personal enrichment. At the same time, Zambian

Part 3: Maintaining Civic Mobilization

society remained relatively demobilized, giving the president the benefit of the doubt and entrusting him with the transition.

There were scattered attempts to bring the corruption and anti-democratic practices of the new administration to light. For instance, journalists from this period describe the *Post* newspaper as a loud voice condemning the new administration for failing to keep its promises. Some members of the original MMD movement also left the government and attempted to form a more democratic opposition. However, these political figures, many of whom were interviewed for this project, reported that these efforts largely failed to have a significant impact since ordinary people remained supportive of President Chiluba.

Having become so deeply enamored with power, President Chiluba also became terrified of losing it. In the lead-up to Zambia's 1996 presidential election, in which he was running for a second term, President Chiluba engaged in a mixture of repression and co-optation that would have been quite familiar in the non-democratic regime that he so vigorously challenged a decade earlier. The government bought off some opposition figures with promises of small numbers of guaranteed seats in the parliament and economic benefits if they would stop challenging the MMD. Others, most prominently the remaining members of the old ruling party, UNIP, faced severe repression, including the arrest and attempted assassination of former President Kenneth Kaunda.

Only after 10 years in power, when people lost faith in President Chiluba and began to mobilize against him, was an effective democratic check put into place. In 2001, Chiluba attempted to subvert the new constitution and run for a third presidential term. Civil society and opposition political forces saw this move as one step too far, a move leading Zambia straight into authoritarianism. They mobilized on a massive scale to prevent it from happening. This time, after a decade of failed promises of change, the Zambian people were responsive to the calls to defend democratic gains and joined the movement against the third term. This mobilization, in turn, successfully pressured members of President Chiluba's party to turn against him, forcing him not to seek a third term.

As this case shows, charismatic and popular leaders are a double-edged sword for civil resistance transitions. On the one hand, their popularity may enable them to engage in important reforms. However, it can also undermine effective mechanisms of grassroots political control. The important lesson for movements is thus neither complete cynicism nor blind faith in their leaders. Leaders should be carefully evaluated based on what they have actually accomplished and criticized clearly and honestly when they fail to keep their promises.

One key aspect of making sure leaders are held to account is in carefully guarding protections for free expression, particularly a free and open press. As shown in the Chiluba case, it is the decisions of ordinary people to support civic mobilization against corrupt leaders that can make the key difference. And for ordinary people to be mobilized, they must be made aware of any abuses or departures from the democratic path that previously idealistic leaders may have engaged in once in power.

> *Movements with negative visions based on what they are against have little to tell their followers about what to strive for once they succeed.*

Maintaining a Democratic Vision of the Future

The movements that succeeded most dramatically in maintaining mobilization during the political transition were those in which organizers worked hard to build a vision of the future that would continue to motivate people to participate in shaping the new political system. People are often motivated to engage in resistance because of the things they reject and want to dismantle. But a core insight, going back to Mohandas Gandhi, is that this kind of negative mobilization is not enough. Movements with negative visions based on what they are against have little to tell their followers about what to strive for once they succeed. Instead, their participants enter a vacuum where they make sacrifices to remove a dictatorship but know little about what to do next.

What is central for movements to keep in mind is that there is a huge gap between getting rid of the old system and establishing the new one. One does not simply flow logically from the other. Establishing a democratic system involves a complex, lengthy, and sometimes very difficult process of decision-making about the country's new system.

Political, social, and economic elites will already be invested in shaping the new regime based on their own vision of the future, which may be different from the needs and desires of ordinary people. Absent the pressure of the masses, elites will shape the new politics in their own image. So it's the people's responsibility, throughout the transition, to remind movement leaders of the collective vision for future democracy.

But how can movements turn a negative vision (one that focuses on the downfall of a regime) into a positive, forward-looking vision of democratic government and society?

Specific strategies will vary depending on a country's circumstances, but we can glean a few general lessons from the successes and failures of past transitions. For instance, working out specifics of what people in the movement want the new political system to look like well before the political breakthrough occurs can provide an important foundation for maintaining a vision of the future past the breakdown of the old regime.

One technical area with major practical consequences is the constitutional system, which outlines exactly what the future democracy will look like. What does democracy mean to the people in the movement, and what kinds of core institutional arrangements could ensure that such a democracy can be achieved? What rights and freedoms have motivated people to engage in the costly action of civil resistance, and how can activists and political leaders blend them into a comprehensive vision of a new political regime? How can activists ensure that political power is not concentrated and abused again and that corruption among the incoming new political class is effectively limited? Concerns with justice for past abuses are often an area to focus on as well (such as truth and reconciliation processes).

Activists, opposition leaders, and ordinary people will have their own priorities, so movement leaders should be careful not to apply a "one-size-fits-all" solution to their vision of a new democratic future. Instead, vision shaping should be deeply local, focused on the needs and desires of the ordinary people whose political engagement during the transition will be crucial for broadening the inclusiveness of politics and ensuring the creation of a new democracy. The key issue is to be thinking—during the struggle and well before a movement succeeds—about this positive vision of a new future.

The movement against the military regime in **Brazil** provides a good example of this process at work. In Brazil, most of the movements that continued to mobilize people painted the 1985 transition not as an endpoint but as a beginning. The new Brazil was more than just about changing political leaders. It was also a matter of creating a set of political institutions that would fundamentally change the nature of political power in Brazil. One activist interviewed for this project described a conference that

brought together activists, at a time when military dictatorship was still firmly in place, to discuss the future of science in Brazil. Instead of framing their discussion around: "It's not possible to accomplish anything until the dictatorship is gone, let's get rid of the dictatorship," they framed it around what they would do once the dictatorship was gone. In a context of greater political freedom, what goals, strategies, and changes would they want to accomplish?

Similarly, Brazil had a robust women's movement that fought against the dictatorship, but also painted the dictatorship as simply one part of a larger, conservative, patriarchal system that they would need to continue opposing even after military rule was gone.

The Brazilian labor movement, both in independent unions and in the new Workers Party (PT), also planned a comprehensive agenda of pushing forward progressive labor provisions in Brazil's new constitution. Old elites heavily opposed this, instead wanting to maintain a quiescent working class in the new democratic system. The military in particular, which had ruled Brazil for the previous two decades, was viscerally opposed to any concessions to the labor movement (Hunter 1997). However, leaders such as future president Lula da Silva argued that simply eliminating military rule was far from their only goal, and that it would be meaningless unless the new democratic practices diverged significantly from past patterns of political and economic elite dominating workers.

The labor movement thus pushed for several extensive protections for workers to be included in Brazil's 1988 constitution. Perhaps the most important and far-reaching of these was a constitutionally guaranteed right to strike, though workers also gained significant concessions in limiting the length of the work week while gaining overtime pay, pensions, and political autonomy for unions (Martinez-Lara 1996, 123-24). They were able to achieve these gains primarily through creating broad cross-union alliances during the ongoing transition that could speak with a single voice in the forum of Brazil's constitutional assembly. Over 350 unions came together to form the Interunion Department for Legislative Advising (DIAP) which pooled their core interests. They were able to coerce politicians who did not agree with their agenda with the potential for mass mobilization if their demands were not met.

This long-term transformative vision drove the Brazilian movement both in its struggle against the military dictatorship and well after the generals had left the presidential palace. Brazil's transition put in place a democratic political regime that went well beyond the bare democratic minimum and instead included many robust protections for the rights and privileges of ordinary people. The vision has not been fully implemented, as seen in the country's recent political scandals, but it continues to motivate a culture of sustained activism that is still pushing the country in a democratic direction.

Conclusion

This chapter has argued that one key challenge in ensuring that the nonviolent overthrow of a dictator leads to democracy is to ensure that the people who struggled to change the old regime continue to push for positive change in the transition to the new system. For nonviolent resistance to effectively push democracy forward, activism must continue past the peak moment of ousting the old government into the uncertain times of transition.

How can movements maintain mobilization and be most effective in ensuring democratic progress? They can seek to be independent, skeptical, and vision-driven. When activists are too close to new political leaders or international donors, when they put too much trust in the good faith of the people who led them against the old regime, or when their vision of the future that united the opposition is limited to removing the authoritarian system, then mobilization will suffer.

The application of these lessons will vary significantly depending on a country's context, and activists should use careful interpretation and rigorous strategic analysis. Yet the underlying principle—that widespread social mobilization is crucial for establishing democracy in civil resistance transitions—should be taken deeply to heart by all those seeking to achieve democratic change through nonviolent resistance.

Part 4
Avoiding Street Radicalism

Maintaining mobilization is a key challenge for continuing to push countries in a civil resistance transition toward democracy. But sometimes, even when mobilization continues, movements incur yet another challenge: relying too much on extra-institutional political action, which undermines the stability of new political institutions. This is where street radicalism enters the analysis.

How street radicalism comes about relates very closely to the mechanisms through which nonviolent resistance positively affects a country's level of democracy. The experience of a successful civil resistance campaign can be highly empowering for the leaders of social and political forces able to mobilize the mass numbers necessary to achieve success (Sharp 1973). However, by its nature, civil resistance involves going outside of the bounds of institutional politics in ways that are disruptive. Such disruption can be extremely powerful in ending political oppression. On a more basic level, it can be used as a powerful tool to shift the balance of political power.

In the weakly institutionalized setting of a transition from authoritarian rule, the forces that came together to oust the previous regime may be tempted to over-rely upon this particularly powerful tool to further their own interests. This may not align with and can, in fact, contradict the public good in a newly emerging democracy. In many cases, this leads to a radicalization of politics, a constant move to the streets when electoral outcomes or government policies fail to satisfy the demands of specific political forces.

Street radicalism takes many different forms depending on the political and social dynamics of a country. Therefore, it is important to highlight the distinctive characteristics of this phenomenon, and, in particular, what separates it from healthy, democracy-supporting forms of civic mobilization and engagement described in the previous chapter. Table 4.1 on page 59 lays out some of these distinctions.

Table 4.1: Distinctions between Street Radicalism and Civic Mobilization

	CIVIC MOBILIZATION	STREET RADICALISM
Basis for Unity	Inclusive and diverse coalitions with public interest	Exclusive, sectoral groups with private interests
Primary Tactics	Pressure mainly, though not exclusively, through engagements within political institutions	Pressure through disruptive actions undertaken outside of political institutions
Attitudes toward Politics	Regular, limited competition	Winner-take-all struggles
Goals	Long-term power transformation	Short-term power-holding

Healthy civic mobilization differs from street radicalism along four key dimensions: the basis for unity, primary tactics, attitude towards politics, and goals. With regard to the basis for unity, in civic mobilization, coalitions maintain diversity and inclusiveness by bringing together various different groups united around general and specific public goals, including responsible and effective governance, accountability of political and administrative elites, or fighting corruption. On the other hand, street radicalism emerges when involved groups are sectoral and exclusive in their membership and advance private interests focused on maintaining or advancing their own privileges and rights.

As for tactics, civic mobilization that supports democratization operates by putting organized pressure on new leaders to remain accountable to their promises. It involves activating people to participate in the emerging avenues of politics. It can certainly involve elements of disruption and withdrawal of support and cooperation when leaders fail to live up to their promises. However, its primary tactical focus is on positive engagement and participation directed toward new and reformed state institutions. In contrast, in street radicalism the tactical focus is typically much more on using the tools of noncooperation and disruption in the form of street presence, to directly attack or impose costs on some competing group.

The tactical repertoires of these two phenomena are different because of their distinct attitudes toward politics. In healthy civic mobilization, political goals are pursued as part of a regular, limited form of competition. Movements, pressure groups, and political parties may sometimes win and sometimes lose, but their political engagement rests on a foundational shared understanding of the boundaries of acceptable political behavior. In contrast, in transitions characterized by street radicalism, the various political groups competing against one another see themselves as engaged in winner-take-all struggles in which one side's victory means the other side's total and complete defeat. Since this is the attitude toward politics, it is only natural that the most extreme tactics are justified to achieve one's goals. This is why street radicalism can also lead to violence.

Democratization is more likely if political or identity group leaders avoid street radicalism and instead begin to develop formal political institutions.

Finally, healthy civic mobilization focuses on goals of long-term diffusion and redistribution of political power, while street radicalism tends to focus on short-term competition over which a particular group will hold political power at a particular moment.

Democratization is more likely if political or identity group leaders avoid street radicalism and instead begin to develop formal political institutions. Pursuing the path of civic mobilization transforms political competition from a winner-take-all struggle (in which the most extreme tactics can be justified) to a regular arena in which competition is limited by widely-accepted rules and norms. Political actors in the latter context are more willing to accept uncertainty in outcomes, including potential failure and an obligation to make compromises with other actors involved in the transition. Changing the political context in this way then pushes new democratic politics forward.

Many different types of actors can carry out street radicalism. In societies deeply divided along ethnic or religious lines, these points of identity cleavage often become the touchstones for competing radicalism, sometimes mixed with violent elements. An example of this is Kenya following the fight for restoration of multiparty democracy in the 1990s.[27] Alternatively, political parties led by particularly charismatic individuals may become the centers of street radicalism, as in Bangladesh following the ouster of President Ershad (Schaffer 2002). And in some cases, both political parties and identity-based groups may serve as the basis for radicalism, as in Madagascar in the early 2000s (Marcus 2004).

Part 4: Avoiding Street Radicalism

All of these cases resulted in political systems in which the forms of democratic politics exist, but their legitimacy and effectiveness fall short of genuine democratic rule. The loser rarely, if ever, accepts electoral outcomes, and the ability to inflict costs through action on the streets becomes the primary tool of political contention.

The specific contours of contention vary depending on political actors' capacity to impose costs. When the balance of forces is fairly even, power change among such groups will be frequent. This has been the case in Thailand, where from 2006 to 2014 the primarily urban Yellow and primarily rural Red factions engaged in several back and forth resistance campaigns, often succeeding in achieving power but never moving from its temporary achievement to a consolidation of power and institutionalization of alternation in power. Eventually, this political instability and radicalism played into the hands of the military, which seized political power in 2014.

In cases where one group possesses significantly more mobilization capacity than another, alternations in power are less likely, but because the institutional mechanisms for loyal opposition are either non-existent or lack legitimacy and influence, politics remains fractious. The dominant group relies on more directly coercive mechanisms to suppress dissent, and the weaker group attempts to undermine the dominant group's position by constant disruptive street actions. This political dynamic, for example, characterized the relationship between the Morsi government in Egypt and the liberal opposition from 2012 to 2013, ultimately motivating the liberal opposition to seek military support to oust Morsi in the 2013 coup.

Analysis of the Civil Resistance Transitions data supports the idea of the pernicious character of street radicalism. In a model of the predicted level of democracy at the end of a civil resistance-initiated political transition (see Figure 4.1 on page 62), street radicalism is a highly significant negative predictor of the level of post-transition democracy. This means that as the level of street radicalism increases, the level of democracy at the end of the transition decreases, controlling for other common explanations of democracy.[28]

Moving from a very low level of street radicalism to a very high level during the transition leads to a predicted drop in the level of democracy at the end of the transition of almost 0.4. This is a very substantial drop—roughly equivalent to the difference in democratic quality between the United States and Iraq in 2016.

Figure 4.1: Street Radicalism in Civil Resistance Transitions and Post-Transition Democracy[29]

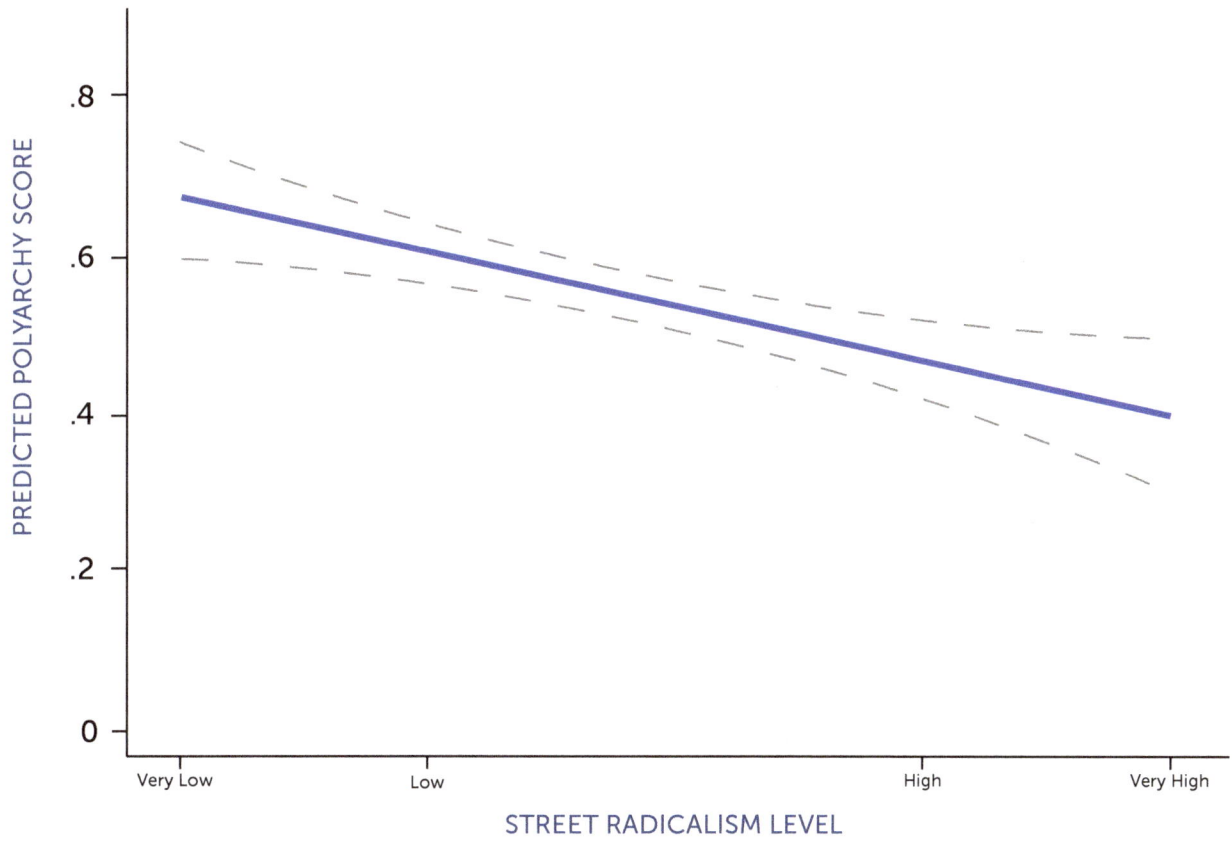

What lessons can movements learn about how to prevent street radicalism and the outcome of fractious politics? As in the previous chapter, this chapter highlights three key lessons:

1. Avoid Extreme Protest Tactics that May Backfire
2. Support Institutional Political Channels
3. Don't Shut Everyone from the Old Regime Out

Avoid Extreme Protest Tactics that May Backfire

In some political transitions, the major challenge is that people have become demobilized and given too much room for anti-democratic elites to derail the move towards democracy. The opposite is actually a challenge as well.

While nonviolent resistance movements have much higher levels of participation than violent resistance movements, the nature of resistance in general is that a relatively smaller number of people will be actively involved in comparison to the number of people who are not. The majority of the population does not participate in moves to the streets, and instead are concerned with more ordinary, bread and butter concerns like finding jobs, providing for their families, and achieving old age in a more prosperous position than they started. Many of the most powerful methods of nonviolent resistance achieve their leverage in part because they affect (and impose costs on) everyone. The best example of this is the general strike. In many ways, the general strike is the "nuclear option" of a nonviolent resistance movement. In a general strike a movement completely shuts down the economic life of a city, region, or entire country. In essence, the movement provokes a crisis that ordinary people cannot ignore because it has such devastating consequences on their lives.

In situations of extreme duress, or when fighting for fundamental freedoms that are widely supported throughout the populace, the disruptive character of nonviolent resistance can enjoy broad public approval and can thus be extremely effective in disrupting oppressive power structures. At the same time, the disruptive character of resistance always involves some risk. Resistance may increase support for a movement, but if the disruption is perceived by the wider populace as unjustified then it can rebound against it.

The transition in **Nepal** is an important example of this dynamic at work. The 2006 movement that overthrew King Gyanendra successfully deployed a very effective set of civil resistance tactics, including a general strike, road blockades around the country, and protesters that numbered in the millions. The scale and disruptiveness of the movement were effective in pressuring the king to step down from power.

However, after the movement ended, this tactical repertoire still continued to play a major role in Nepali politics. Various political forces in Nepal, from the country's major political parties to groups advocating for ethnic, caste, and other minority group rights, continued to use tactics that disrupted public life and imposed heavy economic costs on their opponents. Two of the methods that became quite common were the *bandh*, or general strike, and the *chakka jam*, or traffic jam.

Perhaps the most extreme example of this kind of action was activists from the Madhesh region of southern Nepal blockading roads from India into Nepal. This prevented the importation of many of the basic goods necessary for daily life in Nepal's major urban centers. The Madheshis used this tactic twice—once in 2007 and once in 2015. It proved very effective: The economic pressure successfully led the Nepali political elite to offer substantial concessions, but it significantly turned public opinion against Madheshis and their struggle for equal rights.

The blockade and other disruptive tools of nonviolent resistance used by various political and ethnic groups in Nepal undermined support for democracy as well. In interviews conducted for this monograph, many Nepali political and social leaders, including some who had played key roles in the 2006 revolution, described how the events of the 10 years since the 2006 revolution had undermined their belief in democracy's capacity to meet Nepalis' social and economic needs. A few called for the return of the country's monarchy,[30] while others expressed support for military rule or some other form of strong authoritarian control for a period of time to discipline the country's political system and its civic forces.

It remains to be seen whether any powerful political actor will attempt such full-scale anti-democratic moves. However, what is not in doubt is that relying on these kinds of street actions has severely disrupted the country's democratic transition. This has lengthened the process of establishing a new constitution, undermined the potential for economic growth,[31] and weakened the legitimacy and credibility of political and civil society groups that ousted the monarchy in the name of democratic principles. This has led the Nepali public to become skeptical and cynical about politics and political engagement.

Support Institutional Channels of Politics

It can be difficult for rebels who have been fighting the political system to begin to play the political game. However, making this move is crucial for a new democracy to consolidate and build institutions that can sustain positive change in the long term.

Part 4: Avoiding Street Radicalism

The great innovation of democratic political systems is the blend of conflict and consensus that, in theory, leads to the greatest representation of people's interests. Conflict is unavoidable because of the diversity present in all societies. Any political consensus that completely ignores conflict will almost definitely do so by silencing the voices of the disadvantaged. Yet conflicts without some kind of consensus about how one should resolve them easily spiral out into destruction and violence. Political institutions—that is to say, regular formal or informal rules of the political game—allow necessary social and political conflicts to occur but prevent this escalatory spiral. Instead of easily becoming all-or-nothing struggles between sworn enemies, institutions shift political conflicts into areas of limited competition between rivals.

Political institutions are also crucial for achieving long-term social and economic benefits. Political institutions regulate and center the expectations of political actors, enabling them to focus on long-term goals. When political power contenders know clearly how to get power, what elections will look like, and what the guardrails of political behavior may be, they can easily focus on a wide array of political questions: How can our country achieve economic growth? How can we improve the livelihoods of the underprivileged? What kind of reforms in health, education, and public welfare will be most beneficial for the country?

Constitutions are one of the most important ways of regulating political competition in a democratic system. During political transitions, civil resistance activists should focus on supporting the establishment of a constitutional system acceptable to all major political forces in society. Both the written constitution itself and its drafting process are important areas of concern, since the latter may be a lengthy, involved endeavor.

Still, the written constitution alone will achieve little if political actors do not embrace the norms that inform the constitution. In Nepal, many activists and political elites spoke very highly of the country's constitution, which contains numerous highly progressive and admirable clauses. However, the principles of the constitution have not yet been engrained in political practice, and thus its power to regulate political competition and free up political leaders to focus on bringing benefits to their constituents is limited.

The key function of political institutions is to create the regular, limited forms of competition that make possible productive, sustainable democratic politics. Without them, winner-take-all politics will dominate and undermine political stability. Movements should identify concrete ways to reward political leaders, parties, and the public at large for accepting informal norms and behaviors that regularize political competition, for instance through encouraging dialogue or holding marches in favor of the acceptance of new political rules.

Some individuals and groups within movements should also consider how best they themselves can transition into regular political competition. While it is important to keep outside, independent sources of pressure, as described in the previous chapter, there is a place for some organizations to transition from criticizing the system of political competition to becoming a part of that system.

The move to "institutional" politics should by no means be interpreted as a move to purely "elite" politics in which important decisions are left to people in power. Constitutional principles can also be practiced on the street. One example is when activists maintain strict codes of nonviolent discipline while they invoke and practice their constitutional rights to freedom of expression, protest, or public assembly.

The Brazilian transition underscores the benefits of moving to institutional politics. Prior to the end of the military regime in 1985, Brazil had a long history of political competition spilling well beyond the boundaries of conventional politics. Political competition had been extensive, fierce, and often violent: The Brazilian Empire was overthrown and an elite-led republic established in 1889, followed later by the 1930 revolution against this republic, and the subsequent back and forth of Brazil's politics in the 1950s and 60s, culminating in the 1964 military coup.

Portions of the Brazilian opposition that had come together to push out the military regime also harbored specific historical legacies of violent, all-or-nothing revolutionary struggle. The Communist Party of Brazil (PCdoB), for example, had been founded in 1962 as a Maoist-style revolutionary group attempting not just to overthrow Brazil's military dictatorship but to establish a one-party Communist dictatorship.

There was also significant resentment from the more radical portions of the Brazilian opposition toward their moderate comrades. The popular mobilization of the 1984 *Diretas Já* movement had, in the eyes of many, particularly in the labor movement, been cut off too quickly. Some believed the more moderate, elite factions of the opposition had been too quick to cut a deal with soft-liners in the military regime. Had the movement continued, many believed they could have achieved a much more dramatic break with the military dictatorship and moved much more quickly toward their democratic hopes (Keck 1992, 220-23).

Part 4: Avoiding Street Radicalism

Some of the Brazilian opposition clearly had the experience and motivation to withdraw from the political institutions being set up during the transition. They were certainly seeking to disrupt the transition to achieve a more radical social and political transformation. However, by and large, even the more radical factions of the Brazilian opposition did not choose to take this course. Instead, they recognized the deeper underlying need for organized rules of competition to regulate Brazil's political system. Rather than breaking down or circumventing those formalizing rules through radical street action, they sought, to the extent possible, to ensure that they had a seat at the table in shaping what those rules would look like.

Groups such as the PCdoB and the Worker's Party (PT) put forth concerted efforts to fully integrate the electoral landscape in Brazil's 1986 parliamentary elections—the first elections in the new non-military (but still not fully democratic) system. The 1986 elections were crucial because the parliament chosen in those elections would also function as a constituent assembly to write Brazil's new constitution. While they were a minority, groups such as the PT successfully gained a seat at the table and then began pushing for change through the venue of the constituent assembly.

The fact that all major factions of Brazil's political class sought to participate in the process of writing the constitution gave the constitution tremendous legitimacy. Within this environment they competed vigorously with one another, clearly showing the strong points of divergence between elites from the old military government and elites who had risen out of the nonviolent opposition to the military regime. Because all agreed on the rules of the game, they were still able to limit the disruptive nature of this competition, confining it within the established institution and instead developing stable, peaceful ways of competing with one another.

Allegiance to the brand new institutional framework of Brazilian democracy proved influential just a few years later, when it became clear that Brazil's first directly elected president since the end of the military regime, Fernando Collor de Mello, was engaged in pervasive nepotism and political corruption. Popular movements demanded his ouster but did so solely by calling for constitutional measures to be implemented—an illustration of the trust in and legitimacy of the young institutions.

This enabled Brazil to weather a crisis that threatened to undermine its democracy, but that in reality strengthened it as social forces gave the new political institutions opportunities to do their work. The Brazilian Congress impeached Collor de Mello strictly following the procedures laid out in the constitution, and his vice president,

Itamar Franco, came to power. Because people bought into and supported the process, President Franco was able to enjoy widespread legitimacy and support, an endorsement that enabled him to embark on major economic and social reforms, such as the famous Plano Real monetary reform that has positively transformed Brazil's economy.

Don't Shut Everyone from the Old Regime Out

One common demand after nonviolent revolutions succeed in ousting an old government is for those previously in power to be held accountable for their actions. Particularly in countries where the old regime ruled through intimidation and terror, the injustices of the past cry out for redress. Some degree of changing power relations is necessary for a successful transition to democracy. Changing the rules of the game but keeping the entirely same group of people in positions of power is unlikely to lead to democratic change.

However, it can also cause severe problems when the new people in power demand extreme changes that fully remove from politics and government institutions all figures from the former regime. This is because, in almost any modern state, including non-democratic regimes, the government will absorb a high percentage of the educated, professional, and politically engaged population. Many of these people, while they may be willing to go along with the practices of a non-democratic regime, do not necessarily share its values. If given the opportunity, they may be ready to accept and participate in democratic politics or as civil servants administering state functions in a new political structure after the non-democratic regime falls.

When a transition begins, many of these figures from the old regime may become supportive of democracy if they see prospects for continuing their political fortunes or professional advancements in the new system. However, if demands for terminating their professional participation become too extreme, it is likely to give this highly skilled and potentially influential part of the population strong incentives to undermine the transition and return to a political arrangement where they have access to power. In fact, research from a wide range of transitions has found that when members of the old regime form political parties and compete in the new democratic system, it helps facilitate stable political competition that can lead to consolidated democracy (Loxton

2015, Gryzmala-Busse 2006, Riedl 2014). In contrast, when there are concentrated efforts to shut out members of the old regime, political competition remains more radicalized.

In addition, while imposing the rule of law to punish old abuses is certainly a major step forward for any new democratic government, vengeance on any and all of those who benefited from the old regime is likely to discourage inclusive democratic politics and instead encourage a new kind of exclusive and discriminatory form of governance.

Events from the transition in Zambia illustrate the potential pitfalls of attempting to unfairly exclude members of the old regime from political competition. Although many figures from the Movement for Multiparty Democracy were originally part of the dictatorial United National Independence Party, once the MMD came into power, their position towards UNIP changed dramatically.

Officials from UNIP, including the former President Kenneth Kaunda, sought to continue to engage in electoral politics. While the MMD under President Chiluba did not make UNIP illegal—which would have been a particularly ironic move for a political party with "multiparty democracy" in its very name—they did seek to use the maximum possible extent of government power to disadvantage UNIP and ensure that its political influence remained marginal.

In particular, President Chiluba readily deployed the Preservation of Public Security Act, a colonial-era piece of legislation that the British used to suppress Zambia's independence movement. The Preservation of Public Security Act requires any public gathering to have the approval of the local police chief. If a meeting goes ahead without this permission, it can be, and frequently is, violently dispersed by security forces. UNIP meeting after UNIP meeting faced such repression.

President Kaunda and UNIP reacted strongly to these actions to exclude members of the old regime. Kaunda began demanding not just political mobilization but widespread civil disobedience, arguing that the MMD government "should be fought in the same way UNIP fought the colonial government" (Ihonvbere 1995, 95). Several UNIP leaders developed the "Zero Option" plan to carry out this fight. The plan laid out steps to overthrow the government prior to the 1996 elections through a combination of fostering divisions within MMD and orchestrating a nationwide campaign of strikes and demonstrations. The plan also called for more sinister attempts to disrupt MMD rule, such as paying unemployed young men to initiate a wave of thefts and other petty crimes in major town centers to create a feeling of chaos and insecurity around the country (Ihonvbere 1995, 99). Security forces discovered the plot before it could be implemented, and the MMD proceeded to arrest 26 UNIP leaders and briefly declare a state of emergency.

The Zero Option episode, as well as the MMD's moves to prevent UNIP from competing in elections, significantly undermined the creation of democratic politics. Instead, it initiated a pattern of political competition in Zambia in which the ruling party used every tool at its disposal to bias the electoral playing field against its opponents, ultimately undermining the creation of truly democratic politics.

Conclusion

This chapter has argued that another central challenge in establishing democracy after successful nonviolent resistance movements is the presence of street radicalism. Democratization becomes more difficult during a political transition when:

1. Movements use tools of nonviolent resistance for winner-take-all struggles;
2. The tactics of that struggle focus on extra-institutional disruption and the imposition of costs; and
3. The goals of those struggles are mostly about immediate political competition rather than the long-term transformation of power.

There is a strong statistical association between high levels of street radicalism and declining levels of democracy at the end of political transitions. The cases of Nepal, Zambia, and Brazil point to three lessons about how to reduce street radicalism and channel mobilization during the transition into means that will encourage democratization.

The first lesson is that extreme tactics, even when nonviolent, can backfire. Too much disruption, particularly when it is focused on the kinds of short-term goals typical of street radicalism, can undermine support for democracy. Specific choices of when disruption will be beneficial and when it will not will vary from case to case, and activists should seek deeper knowledge of their own situation to inform their decisions. The general lesson is a cautionary note to be aware that too much disruption in pursuit of short-term goals has potential downsides.

Part 4: Avoiding Street Radicalism

But when and how can movements direct mobilization to avoid street radicalism? They can shift from street activism to supporting and encouraging participation in new institutions, be it strengthening political parties, joining an electoral process, or actively engaging in the work of a constituent assembly that will draft a new constitution laying out the basic rules for a democratic future.

The third and final lesson is to not shut out everyone who was part of the old regime. Shutting them out can create resentment toward democracy from powerful foes who will be highly motivated and, perhaps, well-placed to disrupt it. Instead, working out ways for people who were involved in the old regime to become invested in democratic politics will help create a broader social and political consensus around a new democracy.

Part 5
Final Takeaways on Civil Resistance and Democratization

Research showing the relative effectiveness of nonviolent resistance can be misinterpreted as meaning that nonviolent resistance—particularly in the extreme case of a movement to overthrow a dictator—is easy. This is definitely not the case. Nonviolent struggles, just like any form of resistance to injustice, face major challenges in mobilizing participants (Tilly 1978), maintaining a united front (Ackerman and DuVall 2005), and keeping their participants from engaging in violence (Pinckney 2016). And then, even if a movement succeeds in overcoming these challenges and ousting a dictatorial government, initiating a political transition and moving toward a new form of politics are major struggles in their own right.

When examining the paths out of authoritarian rule, the clearest way to democracy goes through nonviolent resistance.

As the Nepali saying goes: "The elephant got through but its tail is stuck." It is easy to understand the difficulty of overthrowing a dictatorship. When activists see police with tear gas and rubber bullets, when they watch the dictator on television denouncing instability and foreign influence, the sheer size of the task becomes apparent.

But if resisters are not careful, once they have completed the elephantine task of overthrowing a dictator, they may find themselves with the elephant's tail stuck in the transitional doorway. There are real challenges associated with the less glamorous but no less important stages of resistance once the dictator has vacated the seat in government.

Thus, the message of this monograph is both one of encouragement and one of caution. On the encouraging side, it adds to the growing consensus that nonviolent resistance promotes democratic change. Many different scholars have concluded this finding in a variety of different ways, whether looking at individual cases or large-n statistical analyses. The analysis of the Civil Resistance Transitions data confirms this finding, further adding to our confidence in this highly robust and substantive relationship.

Part 5: Final Takeaways on Civil Resistance and Democratization

When examining the paths out of authoritarian rule, the clearest way to democracy goes through nonviolent resistance.

However, on the cautionary side, it is also clear that nonviolently overthrowing a dictator on its own is not enough to ensure a robust, representative democracy. More challenges arise once the dictator is gone and the country is in the midst of moving toward a new political regime. It is important to recognize these challenges from a scholarly perspective and from an activist and political perspective.

It is also important to recognize the limitations of scholarly knowledge when it comes to something as complex as nonviolent resistance. While strong empirical evidence supports this monograph's lessons, this does not necessarily mean that they will play out in the same way in new cases as they have historically. Activists and policymakers seeking to apply these findings should look first to the dynamics of their own societies and implement these lessons only as they are appropriate in their specific contexts.

The lessons given here are guidelines to enrich the thinking of scholars, activists, and policymakers. They cannot be directly and simplistically applied in any situation. Instead, readers should incorporate them with careful strategic consideration of the different actors at work in a country's politics, the incentives that those actors face, and the underlying political environment.

Takeaways for Scholars

Several findings from this monograph are relevant to the growing academic discussion about nonviolent resistance and democratization. The quantitative modeling in this monograph, based on a pool of more than 300 transitions from authoritarian regimes from 1945 to 2015, has shown, first, that nonviolent resistance as a tactic for initiating regime breakdown strongly increases the likelihood of democratization, controlling for other prominent explanations for democratization. Second, within the population of 78 transitions initiated by nonviolent resistance, high civic mobilization and low street radicalism largely explain the variation in democratic outcomes.

In other words, how non-democratic regimes are ousted has important effects on long-term outcomes. Nonviolent resistance has an independent impact on democratization beyond any connection to other democracy-facilitating factors such as high socio-economic development or a moderate level of authoritarianism. The results of this study underscore these ideas.

This study is also a strong call for scholars to recognize and clearly articulate that different patterns of political behavior during transitional periods will lead to radically different outcomes. This centrally important political process—democratization—involves many different steps, and each step matters. In particular, patterns of behavior related to civic mobilization and patterns of street radicalism have a statistically significant and substantive impact on the level of democracy at the end of a political transition. We must take these into account if we wish to develop a detailed understanding and robust predictive models of democratization.

Finally, this monograph contributes to broader discussions about the relative impact of structural factors and agency-related decisions. Because the impact of these patterns of behavior adds explanatory leverage, this strongly suggests that such patterns cannot simply be derived from their structural preconditions. We should examine patterns of choices made by actors as explanatory factors in their own right and continue to develop models that show that structural factors may shape, but do not determine, major political outcomes.

Takeaways for Civil Resistance Practitioners

From an activist's perspective, the message is to think clearly and carefully about the steps that come after the ouster of a non-democratic regime. Earlier literature on strategic nonviolent conflict calls on activists to think carefully about the steps to achieving the goals of their struggles (Ackerman and Kruegler 1994, Sharp 2005, Helvey 2004). Similarly, this monograph calls on activists to think carefully about what comes after their central goals are achieved, and to do this thinking while they are still engaged in resisting repression and injustice—well before any political opening.

How can activists think through the political visions, organizational structures, and practices of resistance that will continue to push their country's political system toward a democratic, representative future? How can they anticipate and plan for the challenges that are likely to arise along the way?

One useful way to think about these challenges is in terms of mobilization and street radicalism. Continued mobilization and popular pressure play an important role in keeping new political elites accountable and ensuring that the transition away from dictatorship truly goes the full distance to democracy. Yet this mobilization must be careful to avoid the temptations of street radicalism and instead settle for the regular routines of democratic politics.

These challenges are surely not the only ones that arise in civil resistance transitions. Future research may productively articulate many more. Nor is the resolution of these challenges a simple matter of recognizing that they exist. As with any political dynamic, the interacting decisions of many different players come together to create the outcome. Individual activists, new political leaders, social and political elites: all of these various groups will together affect how these challenges play out in individual transitions.

Takeaways for External Actors

How can external actors interested in helping nonviolent movements apply this monograph's lessons? The first way is to exercise more caution. External actors should be careful to give local movements the flexibility and autonomy that will allow them to remain intimately connected to the needs, desires, and passions of their local constituencies. Long-term mobilization is best served by grassroots initiatives from people who understand and are deeply connected to their local context.

However, external actors may play a role in helping activists think through the potential challenges that may arise once they have brought down repressive political regimes. Sharing principles of careful strategic planning, preparation for maintaining mobilization once the old regime is no longer in power to keep people engaged, as well as technical training and preparation for the complex questions of arranging new constitutional structures may all be helpful interventions.

More specifically, external actors can think about suitable strategies, including trainings, knowledge and skills sharing, and capacity building that could help activists address the specific challenges of mobilization and street radicalism. One way of encouraging this capacity building would be through connecting movements in the

midst of political transitions with those who have successfully navigated transitions in the past.

As we see rollbacks in democracy in many places around the world, the promise of nonviolent resistance becomes ever more important. It is the author's hope that this monograph will be a resource for those who are helping to bring that promise to fruition, and a guide along this difficult path—from the moment of hope as the people push a dictator from power, to the moment of fulfillment as the downfall of the old is followed by the creation of a new democratic political order that respects the freedoms and aspirations of the people.

Bibliography

Abramowitz, Michael J. 2018. "Democracy in Crisis: Freedom in the World 2018." Freedom House. Accessed March 5, 2018. https://freedomhouse.org/sites/default/files/FH_FITW_Report_2018_Final_SinglePage.pdf.

Ackerman, Peter, and Christopher Kruegler. 1994. *Strategic Nonviolent Conflict: The Dynamics of People Power in the Twentieth Century*. Westport, CT: Praeger Publishers.

Ackerman, Peter, and Jack DuVall. 2005. "People Power Primed." *Harvard International Review* 27 (2): 42-47.

Almeida, Thamyris F. T. 2015. *Araguaia: Maoist Uprising and Military Counterinsurgency in the Brazilian Amazon, 1967-1975*. Amherst, MA: University of Massachusetts - Amherst (Master's Thesis).

Bayer, Markus, Felix Bethke, and Matteo Dressler. 2017. "How Nonviolent Resistance Helps to Consolidate Gains for Civil Society After Democratization." *Minds of the Movement*. December 12. Accessed January 18, 2018. https://www.nonviolent-conflict.org/blog_post/how-nonviolent-resistance-helps-consolidate-gains-democratization/.

Bayer, Markus, Felix S. Bethke, and Daniel Lambach. 2016. "The Democratic Dividend of Nonviolent Resistance." *Journal of Peace Research* 758-71.

Beissinger, Mark. 2013. "The Semblance of Democratic Revolution: Coalitions in Ukraine's Orange Revolution." *American Political Science Review* 107 (3): 574-92.

Berry, Jeffrey M. 2002. "Validity and Reliability Isues in Elite Interviewing." *PS: Political Science and Politics* 35 (4): 679-82.

Bethke, Felix S., and Jonathan Pinckney. 2016. "Nonviolent Resistance and the Quality of Democracy." *V-Dem Users Working Paper*.

Boix, Carles, Michael Miller, and Sebastian Rosato. 2013. "A Complete Data Set of Political Regimes, 1800-2007." *Comparative Political Studies* 46 (12): 1523-54.

Bratton, Michael, and Nicholas Van de Walle. 1997. *Democratic Experiments in Africa: Regime Transitions in Comparative Perspective*. New York, NY: Cambridge University Press.

Brinks, Daniel, and Michael Coppedge. 2006. "Diffusion is no Illusion: Neighbor Emulation in the Third Wave of Democracy." *Comparative Political Studies* 39 (4): 463-89.

Bunce, Valerie J., and Sharon L. Wolchik. 2011. *Defeating Authoritarian Leaders in Postcommunist Countries*. Cambridge: Cambridge University Press.

Carpenter, R. Charli. 2007. "Setting the Advocacy Agenda: Theorizing Issue Emergence and Nonemergence in Transnational Advocacy Networks." *International Studies Quarterly* 51 (1): 99-120.

Celestino, Mauricio Rivera, and Kristian Skrede Gleditsch. 2013. "Fresh Carnations or all Thorn, no Rose? Nonviolent Campaigns and Transitions in Autocracies." *Journal of Peace Research* 50 (3): 385-400.

Chenoweth, Erica, and Christopher Shay. 2017. "Updating Nonviolent Campaigns: Introducing NAVCO 2.1." *Paper Presented at the American Political Science Association Annual Conference*.

Chenoweth, Erica, and Maria Stephan. 2011. *Why Civil Resistance Works: The Strategic Logic of Nonviolent Resistance*. New York, NY: Columbia University Press.

Cooley, Alexander, and James Ron. 2002. "The NGO Scramble: Organizational Insecurity and the Political Economy of Transnational Action." *International Security* 27 (1): 5-39.

Coppedge, Michael, John Gerring, Staffan I. Lindberg, Svend-Erik Skaaning, Jan Teorell, David Altman, Michael Bernhard, et al. 2017. *V-Dem Codebook v7*. Gothenburg: Varieties of Democracy (V-Dem) Project.

—. 2017. *V-Dem Country-Year Dataset v7*. Gothenburg, Sweden: Varieties of Democracy (V-Dem) Project.

—. 2017. "V-Dem Dataset v7." Varieties of Democracy (V-Dem) Project.

Dahl, Robert. 1973. *Polyarchy: Participation and Opposition*. New Haven, CT: Yale University Press.

Easton, David. 1953. *The Political System*. New York: Alfred A Knopf.

Ekiert, Grzegorz, and Jan Kubik. 2001. *Rebellious Civil Society: Popular Protest and Democratic Consolidation in Poland, 1989-1993*. Ann Arbor, MI: University of Michigan Press.

Fernandes, Tiago. 2015. "Rethinking Pathways to Democracy: Civil Society in Portugal and Spain, 1960s-2000s." *Democratization* 22 (6): 1074-1104.

Finkel, Evgeny, and Yitzhak M. Brudny. 2012. "Russia and the Colour Revolutions." *Democratization* 19 (1): 15-36.

Galtung, Johan. 1969. "Violence, Peace, and Peace Research." *Journal of Peace Research* 6 (3): 167-91.

Garcia-Ponce, Omar, and Leonard Wantchekon. 2017. "Critical Junctures: Independence Movements and Democracy in Africa." *Working Paper*. Accessed September 27, 2017. https://scholar.princeton.edu/sites/default/files/lwantche/files/insurgency_140730.pdf.

Bibliography

Geddes, Barbara, Joseph Wright, and Erica Frantz. 2014. "Autocratic Breakdown and Regime Transitions: A New Data Set." *Perspectives on Politics* 12 (2): 313-31.

Gleditsch, Kristian Skrede, and Michael Ward. 2006. "Diffusion and the International Context of Democratization." *International Organization* 60 (4): 911-33.

Goertzel, Ted G. 1999. *Fernando Henrique Cardoso: Reinventing Democracy in Brazil*. Boulder, CO: Lynne Rienner Publishers.

Gryzmala-Busse, Anna. 2006. "Authoritarian Determinants of Democratic Party Competition: The Communist Successor Parties in East Central Europe." *Party Politics* 12 (3): 415-37.

Haber, Stephen, and Victor Menaldo. 2011. "Do Natural Resources Fuel Authoritarianism? A Reappraisal of the Resource Curse." *American Political Science Review* 105 (1): 1-26.

Hadenius, Axel, and Jan Teorell. 2007. "Pathways from Authoritarianism." *Journal of Democracy* 18 (1): 143-57.

Helvey, Robert. 2004. *On Strategic Nonviolent Conflict: Thinking About the Fundamentals*. Boston, MA: The Albert Einstein Institution.

Hendrix, Cullen. 2010. "Measuring State Capacity: Theoretical and Empirical Implications for the Study of Civil Conflict." *Journal of Peace Research* 47 (3): 273-85.

Hughes, Melanie M., Lindsey Peterson, Jill Ann Harrison, and Pamela Paxton. 2009. "Power and Relation in the World Polity: The INGO Network Country Score, 1978-1998." *Social Forces* 87 (4): 1711-42.

Hunter, Wendy. 1997. *Eroding Military Influence in Brazil: Politicians Against Soldiers*. Chapel Hill, NC: University of North Carolina Press.

Ihonvbere, Julius O. 1995. "The 'Zero Option' Controversy in Zambia: Western Double Standards vis a vis Safeguarding Security?" *Africa Spectrum* 30 (1): 93-104.

Johnstad, Petter Grahl. 2010. "Nonviolent Democratization: A Sensitivity Analysis of How Transition Mode and Violence Impact the Durability of Democracy." *Peace & Change* 35 (3): 464-82.

Karatnycky, Adrian, and Peter Ackerman. 2005. *How Freedom is Won: From Civic Resistance to Durable Democracy*. New York, NY: Freedom House.

Keck, Margaret E. 1992. *The Workers' Party and Democratization in Brazil*. New Haven, CT: Yale University Press.

King, Gary, Robert O. Keohane, and Sidney Verba. 1994. *Designing Social Inquiry: Scientific Inference in Qualitative Research*. Princeton, NJ: Princeton University Press.

Kinzo, Maria D'Alva G. 1988. *Legal Opposition Politics under Authoritarian Rule in Brazil: The Case of the MDB, 1966-79*. New York, NY: St. Martin's Press.

Koch, Dirk-Jan, Axel Dreher, Peter Nunnenkamp, and Rainer Thiele. 2009. "Keeping a Low Profile: What Determines the Allocation of Aid by Non-Governmental Organizations." *World Development* 37 (5): 902-18.

Leech, Beth L. 2002. "Asking Questions: Techniques for Semistructured Interviews." *PS: Political Science and Politics* 35 (4): 665-68.

Lehoucq, Fabrice. 2016. "Does Nonviolence Work?" *Comparative Politics* 48 (2): 269-87.

Levitsky, Steven, and Lucan A. Way. 2010. *Competitive Authoritarianism: Hybrid Regimes After the Cold War*. New York, NY: Cambridge University Press.

Li, Eric X. 2014. "The Umbrella Revolution Won't Give Hong Kong Democracy. Protesters Should Stop Calling for It." *The Washington Post*. October 6. Accessed June 19, 2016. https://www.washingtonpost.com/posteverything/wp/2014/10/06/the-umbrella-revolution-wont-give-hong-kong-democracy-protesters-should-stop-calling-for-it/.

Lieberman, Evan S. 2005. "Nested Analysis as a Mixed-Method Strategy for Comparative Research." *The American Political Science Review* 99 (3): 435-52.

Linz, Juan J. 1978. *The Breakdown of Democratic Regimes: Crisis, Breakdown and Reequilibration*. Baltimore, MD: The Johns Hopkins University Press.

Lipset, Seymour Martin. 1959. "Some Social Requisites of Democracy: Economic Development and Political Legitimacy." *American Political Science Review* 53 (1): 69-105.

Loxton, James. 2015. "Authoritarian Successor Parties." *Journal of Democracy* 26 (3): 157-70.

Marcus, Richard R. 2004. "Political Change in Madagascar: Populist Democracy or Neopatrimonialism by Another Name?" *Institute for Security Studies Papers* 89: 1-20.

Marshall, Monty G. 2015. The Polity IV Annual Time-Series, 1800-2014, Dataset. Accessed November 24, 2015. http://www.systemicpeace.org/inscr/p4v2014.xls.

Marshall, Monty G., Ted Robert Gurr, and Keith Jaggers. 2016. *Polity IV Project: Political Regime Characteristics and Transitions, 1800-2015*. Center for Systemic Peace.

Martinez-Lara, Javier. 1996. *Building Democracy in Brazil: The Politics of Constitutional Change, 1985-95*. New York, NY: St. Martin's Press.

Mattaini, Mark. 2013. *Strategic Nonviolent Power: The Science of Satyagraha*. Edmonton: Athabasca University Press.

May, Todd. 2015. *Nonviolent Resistance: A Philosophical Introduction*. Hoboken, NJ: John Wiley & Sons.

McCracken, Grant. 1988. *The Long Interview*. Thousand Oaks, CA: Sage.

Morfit, N. Simon. 2011. "AIDS is Money: How Donor Preferences Reconfigure Local Realities." *World Development* 39 (1): 64-76.

Bibliography

Nepstad, Sharon Erickson. 2011. *Nonviolent Revolutions: Civil Resistance in the Late 20th Century*. New York, NY: Oxford University Press.

O'Donnell, Guillermo, and Philippe Schmitter. 1986. *Transitions from Authoritarian Rule: Tentative Conclusions about Uncertain Democracies*. Baltimore, MD: The Johns Hopkins University Press.

Paxton, Pamela, Melanie M. Hughes, and Nicholas E. Reith. 2015. "Extending the INGO Network Country Score, 1950-2008." *Sociological Science* 2: 287-307.

Pinckney, Jonathan. 2017. *Between Liberation and Freedom: Nonviolent Resistance and Democratization (Unpublished Dissertation)*. Denver, CO: University of Denver.

—. 2016. *Making or Breaking Nonviolent Discipline in Civil Resistance Struggles*. Washington, DC: International Center on Nonviolent Conflict.

—. 2014. *Winning Well: Civil Resistance Mechanisms of Success, Democracy, and Civil Peace*. Denver: University of Denver Master's Thesis.

Pishchikova, Kateryna, and Richard Youngs. 2016. "Divergent and Partial Transitions: Lessons from Ukraine and Egypt." In *Democratization in the 21st Century: Reviving Transitology*, edited by Mohammed-Mahmoud Ould Mohamedou and Timothy Sisk. Abingdon, UK: Taylor & Francis.

Przeworski, Adam. 1991. *Democracy and the Market: Political and Economic Reforms in Eastern Europe and Latin America*. New York, NY: Cambridge University Press.

Rabushka, Alvin, and Kenneth A. Shepsle. 1972. *Politics in Plural Societies: A Theory of Democratic Instability*. Columbus, OH: Charles E. Merrill Publishing.

Rakner, Lise. 2003. *Political and Economic Liberalisation in Zambia, 1991-2001*. Stockholm: The Nordic Africa Institute.

Riedl, Rachel Beatty. 2014. *Authoritarian Origins of Democratic Party Systems in Africa*. New York: Cambridge University Press.

Ritter, Daniel P. 2014. *The Iron Cage of Liberalism: International Politics and Unarmed Revolutions in the Middle East and North Africa*. New York, NY: Oxford University Press.

RT. 2017. "Putin Vows to Prevent 'Color Revolutions' for Russia and its Eurasian Allies." *RT*. April 12. Accessed March 5, 2018. https://www.rt.com/politics/384451-putin-vows-to-prevent-color/.

Schaffer, Howard B. 2002. "Back and Forth in Bangladesh." *Journal of Democracy* 13 (1): 76-83.

Schneider, Ronald M. 1991. *Order and Progress: A Political History of Brazil*. Boulder, CO: Westview Pres.

Schrodt, Philip A., Deborah J. Gerner, Omur Yllmaz, and Dennis Hermreck. 2008. "The CAMEO (Conflict and Mediation Event Observations) Actor Coding Framework." *Annual Meeting of the International Studies Association*.

Schuller, Mark. 2012. *Killing with Kindness: Haiti, International Aid, and NGOs*. New Brunswick, NJ: Rutgers University Press.

Schumpeter, Joseph. 1942. *Capitalism, Socialism and Democracy*. New York, NY: Routledge.

Sharp, Gene. 1973. *The Politics of Nonviolent Action*. Boston, MA: Porter Sargent Publishers.

—. 2005. *Waging Nonviolent Struggle: 20th Century Practice and 21st Century Potential*. Boston, MA: Porter Sargent Publishers.

Shaw, Randy. 1996. *The Activist's Handbook: A Primer for the 1990s and Beyond*. Berkeley, CA: University of California Press.

Shrestha, Min Bahadur, and Shashi Kant Chaudhary. 2014. "The Economic Cost of General Strikes in Nepal." *Nepal Rastra Bank Economic Review* 26 (1): 1-23. Accessed August 15, 2017. https://www.nrb.org.np/ecorev/pdffiles/vol26-1_art1.pdf.

Spradley, James P. 1979. *The Ethnographic Interview*. New York, NY: Holt, Rinehart, and Winston.

Squier, John. 2002. "Civil Society and the Challenge of Russian Gosudarstvennost." *Demokratizatsiya* 10 (2): 166-82.

Teles, Janaina de Almeida. 2017. "The Araguaia Guerrilla War (1972 - 1974): Armed Resistance to the Brazilian Dictatorship." *Latin American Perspectives* 44 (5): 30-52.

Teorell, Jan. 2010. *Determinants of Democratization: Explaining Regime Change in the World, 1972-2006*. New York, NY: Cambridge University Press.

Tilly, Charles. 1978. *From Mobilization to Revolution*. Reading, MA: Addison-Wesley.

Tucker, Joshua A. 2007. "Enough! Electoral Fraud, Collective Action Problems, and Post-Communist Colored Revolutions." *Perspectives on Politics* 5 (3): 535-51.

Vinthagen, Stellan. 2015. *A Theory of Nonviolent Action: How Civil Resistance Works*. London, UK: Zed Books.

Zunes, Stephen. 2018. *Civil Resistance Against Coups: A Comparative and Historical Perspective*. Washington, DC: ICNC Press.

Methodological Appendix

This methodological appendix describes in greater detail the research methods used to generate findings described in this monograph. It also provides reference materials and more detailed reports of those findings. It is geared more toward scholarly audiences curious about the research than it is toward general audiences. However, general audience readers curious about the research may also find much that is of interest.

The first section of the methodological appendix describes the statistical methods behind the results presented at the end of Chapter 2 and the beginning of Chapters 3 and 4. The second section describes the qualitative methods behind the case study material presented in support of the lessons learned primarily in Chapters 3 and 4.

Quantitative Research

In this section of the methodological appendix, I provide more detail on how the variables included in the quantitative testing were coded.

Civil Resistance Transitions

The first key element to consider is how to set up the population of political transitions, and whether a particular transition can be considered a civil resistance transition. As described in Chapter 1, the population of cases, both of transitions as a whole and then of civil resistance transitions (CRTs), comes from combining two well-respected data sources: the data on non-democratic regimes and their types of failure produced by Barbara Geddes, Joseph Wright, and Erica Frantz (2014), and the NAVCO 2.1 dataset produced by Erica Chenoweth and Christopher Shay.

The Geddes data includes every instance in which an authoritarian regime broke down. It has a crucial advantage over other data sources because it measures the duration of individual regimes, defined as "the rules that: (1) identify the group from which leaders can come; and (2) determine who influences leadership choice and policy" (Geddes, Wright and Frantz 2014, 314). Transitions from one authoritarian regime to another are captured in the data, even if the level of democracy remained more or less unchanged from before the transition to after the transition. For instance, the Cuban Revolution in 1959 or the Iranian Revolution in 1979, in which one authoritarian regime was replaced by another, are both captured in the data as transitions from one regime to another rather than continuous periods of non-democracy.

The population of transitions began with the entire population of authoritarian regime breakdown from 1945 through 2011 in the Geddes data. All of the transitions from colonial rule to independence during this time period were also added. This process leads to a total population of 331 transitions.

The number of CRTs was then determined from this population. The first step in this process was to identify all country-years with ongoing nonviolent resistance campaigns in NAVCO 2.1 that correlated with a year of authoritarian regime breakdown in the Geddes data.[33] Each of these cases was then checked individually through an examination of the country-specific scholarly literature. A small number of cases discovered through independent research and through examining the cases included in Pinckney (2014) and Bethke and Pinckney (2016) were also added.

To determine whether a case warranted inclusion as a CRT depended on four key factors:

1. *Scope*. Was the civil resistance campaign of a size and ubiquity that it would have been almost impossible to ignore? Larger campaigns that were spread more widely across the country are more likely to have had a crucial impact on the subsequent process of political development. Campaigns that took place concurrently with regime transitions but were small or concentrated solely in isolated pockets of the country were treated with more skepticism.

2. *Sporadic reference in the literature*. If in reviewing the secondary literature on a case where a civil resistance movement took place one routinely finds the civil resistance campaign is ignored, or its significance downplayed by scholars and other observers, then its inclusion was treated with greater skepticism.

3. *Time elapsed*. If regime breakdown occurred coterminous with, or in the immediate aftermath of, major civil resistance activity, then the case was considered a more likely candidate for inclusion. If a long period of time elapsed between major nonviolent resistance activities and the regime change, then the case was considered more skeptically.

4. *Counterfactual plausibility*. This is the most powerful criterion, even if it is also the most abstract. Can one make a plausible case that the trajectory of regime breakdown would have occurred in the same or a similar way absent the civil resistance campaign? If so, then the case is likely not suitable for inclusion as a CRT. If, however, the historical case for regime change is difficult to plausibly imagine absent the civil resistance campaign, then the case is likely a CRT.

Table AP.1 on pages 86 through 88 lists all CRTs included in the study, along with their corresponding start year and country.

Table AP.1: Full List of Civil Resistance Transitions

Country	Year	Campaign Name
Guatemala	1945	October Revolutionaries
India	1947	Gandhian Campaign
Haiti	1956	
Ghana	1957	Convention People's Party movement
Colombia	1958	Anti-Rojas
Venezuela	1958	Anti-Jimenez
Democratic Republic of Congo	1960	
South Korea	1960	South Korea Student Revolution
Cameroon	1961	Cameroon anti-colonialist movement
Dominican Republic	1962	Anti-Balaguer
Zambia	1964	Zambia Anti-occupation
Malawi	1964	Nyasaland African Congress
Sudan	1965	
Madagascar	1972	Anti-Tsiranana Campaign
Thailand	1973	Thai student protests
Portugal	1974	Carnation Revolution
Greece	1974	Greece Anti-Military
Bolivia	1979	Bolivian Anti-Junta
Iran	1979	Iranian Revolution
Bolivia	1982	Bolivian Anti-Junta
Argentina	1983	Argentina pro-democracy movement
Uruguay	1984	Uruguay Anti-Military
Brazil	1985	Diretas Ja
Sudan	1985	Anti-Jaafar
Haiti	1986	Anti-Duvalier
Philippines	1986	People Power
South Korea	1987	South Korea Anti-Military
Panama	1989	Anti-Noriega
Chile	1989	Anti-Pinochet Movement
East Germany	1989	East Germany pro-dem movement
Poland	1989	Solidarity
Czechoslovakia	1989	Velvet Revolution
Hungary	1990	Hungary pro-dem movement
Bulgaria	1990	Bulgaria Anti-Communist

Table AP.1: Full List of Civil Resistance Transitions *(continued)*

Country	Year	Campaign Name
Benin	1990	Benin Anti-Communist
Mongolia	1990	Mongolian Anti-communist
Bangladesh	1990	Bangladesh Anti-Ershad
Nepal	1990	The Stir
Albania	1991	Albania Anti-Communist
Slovenia	1991	Slovenian Independence
Soviet Union	1991	Russia pro-dem movement
Estonia	1991	Singing Revolution
Latvia	1991	Latvia pro-dem movement
Lithuania	1991	Sajudis
Belarus	1991	Belarus Anti-Communist
Georgia	1991	Georgia Anti-Soviet
Mali	1991	Mali Anti-Military
Niger	1991	Niger Anti-Military
Zambia	1991	Zambia Anti-Single Party
Kyrgyzstan	1991	Kyrgyzstan Democratic Movement
Guyana	1992	Anti Burnham/Hoyte
Thailand	1992	Thai pro-dem movement
Nigeria	1993	Nigeria Anti-Military
Central African Republic	1993	
Madagascar	1993	Active Forces
Malawi	1994	Anti-Banda
South Africa	1994	South Africa Second Defiance Campaign
Nigeria	1999	Nigeria Anti-Military
Indonesia	1999	Anti-Suharto
Mexico	2000	Anti-PRI
Peru	2000	Anti-Fujimori
Croatia	2000	Croatian Institutional Reform
Serbia	2000	Anti-Milosevic
Senegal	2000	Anti-Diouf
Ghana	2000	
Lesotho	2002	
Madagascar	2002	Madagascar pro-democracy movement
East Timor	2002	

Table AP.1: Full List of Civil Resistance Transitions *(continued)*

Country	Year	Campaign Name
Georgia	2003	Rose Revolution
Ukraine	2004	Orange Revolution
Lebanon	2005	Cedar Revolution
Kyrgyzstan	2005	Tulip Revolution
Liberia	2006	
Nepal	2006	Nepalese Anti-government
Pakistan	2008	Lawyer's Movement
Tunisia	2011	Anti-Ben Ali Campaign (Jasmine Revolution)
Egypt	2011	Anti-Mubarak Movement
Yemen	2011	Anti-Saleh Movement

Democracy Source and Coding

The sources for coding democracy, both in a continuous and binary sense, are described in the main text and thus not repeated in depth here. Democracy as a continuous variable is coded using the polyarchy score from the Varieties of Democracy project. Democracy in a binary sense is coded primarily using the coding of democratic regimes from the Geddes et al 2014 data. Countries that were not included in the Geddes dataset were coded using the Boix, Miller and Rosato dataset of democratic regimes (Boix, Miller and Rosato 2013).

Civic Mobilization and Street Radicalism

When operationalizing the two concepts introduced in this monograph: civic mobilization and street radicalism, rather than relying on a single empirical indicator, primary factor analysis is used to capture both phenomena as underlying latent dimensions that are imperfectly captured by several different observable indicators. It is important to note that while some of the indicators used to construct these factors come from the Varieties of Democracy project, none of them are components in the polyarchy index, which is one of the primary dependent variables. Factor analysis uses the patterns of covariance between different empirical indicators to describe the underlying dimensionalities that they share. The central idea is that certain factors we are interested in, in this case civic mobilization and street radicalism, cannot be directly measured. However, several different factors that we can measure are related to the one we can't measure. Thus we can get a good idea of what the unmeasurable factor is like by combining the measurable factors based on their patterns of change.

Civic mobilization is measured by combining three different indicators, all of which were averaged across the period of transition. The first indicator, from the Varieties of Democracy project, measures the degree of popular involvement in civil society activity in a country in a year. The coding of this variable involved asking the expert coders to characterize a country's level of public involvement in civil society on a four-point scale ranging from a characterization of "most associations are state-sponsored...participation is not purely voluntary" at one end to "there are many diverse CSOs and it is considered normal for people to be at least occasionally active in one of them" at the other end (Coppedge, Gerring, et al. 2017, 246).

The second indicator measures the degree of public deliberation. As with the above measure, country experts coded this variable based on an ordinal characterization of a country in a year. Codings could range on a six-point scale from values equivalent to "public deliberation is never allowed" to "large numbers of non-elite groups as well as ordinary people tend to discuss major policies among themselves, in the media, in associations or neighborhoods, or in the streets. Grass roots deliberation is common and unconstrained" (Coppedge, Gerring, et al. 2017, 202-203).

The two measures from V-Dem capture more institutional forms of mobilization. A measure from the Phoenix Event Data Set from the Cline Center at the University of Illinois captures more traditionally considered nonviolent resistance. It is a sum of the number of "protest" events in a country in a year, according to the CAMEO ontology (Schrodt, et al. 2008), with adjustments made to account for temporal and geographic reporting bias. This is a fairly broad category of events that includes sub-categories such as "rally or demonstrate," "conduct strike or boycott," and "obstruct or block passage."

When run through principal factor analysis, these three measures combine to create a single factor above the common standard of an eigenvalue greater than one, strongly suggesting that their covariance can be best explained in terms of a single underlying dimension. Table AP.2 below shows the factor loading of the indicators, averaged across the five Amelia imputations. As the table shows, the Phoenix measure loads weakest onto the factor, meaning that this indicator is less strongly associated with the other two indicators than they are with each other. This reflects the pact that protests are a slightly different form of mobilization. However, the factor analysis does not generate a second factor with an eigenvalue above one, indicating that there is not a strong second dimension to these indicators.

Table AP.2: Civic Mobilization Component Factor Loading

Variable	Factor Loading
Public Deliberation	0.791795
Civil Society Participation	0.792332
Protest Events	0.045711

Methodological Appendix

The street radicalism factor similarly uses some variables from V-Dem as well as one from the Polity IV dataset to generate its factor score, with all variables similarly averaged across the transitional period. The first measures the degree to which political actors engage in electoral boycotts, reflecting political polarization and a lack of trust in new institutions. This is a four-level ordinal variable that ranges from "no parties or candidates boycotted the elections" to "all opposition parties and candidates boycotted the elections" and is then transformed into a continuous variable using V-Dem's ordinal interval response theory method (Coppedge, Gerring, et al. 2017, 96-97).

The second measures the degree to which electoral results are accepted and is also a four-level ordinal variable transformed into a continuous variable through interval response theory methods. The variable's original values ranged from "no candidates accepted the results of the election" to "all parties and candidates accepted the results" (Coppedge, Gerring, et al. 2017, 107). The third measures the degree to which "anti-system" movements, defined as "any movement – peaceful or armed – that is based in the country (not abroad) and is organized in opposition to the current political system" are present in the political system and has original values that range from "anti-system movements are practically non-existent" to "there is a very high level of anti-system movement activity, posing a real and present threat to the regime" (Coppedge, Gerring, et al. 2017, 247).

A measure from the Polity IV dataset based on their "regulation of participation" or parreg variable is also included. In Polity's codebook, this variable is presented as ordinal with five possible levels, capturing a political system's place along the spectrum of "unregulated" to "regulated." Regulation of participation can capture any number of diverse aspects of the political system and does not precisely connect to the concept of street radicalism. However, one level of this variable is intended to capture whether a political system is "sectarian," that is, according to the Polity IV codebook, a political system where "political demands are characterized by incompatible interests and intransigent posturing among multiple identity groups and oscillate more or less regularly between intense factionalism and government favoritism" (Marshall, Gurr and Jaggers, Polity IV Project: Political Regime Characteristics and Transitions, 1800-2015 2016, 26). This description closely approximates a political system characterized by street radicalism, so I created a binary transformation of the parreg variable capturing whether a country was considered "sectarian" in a year.

As with the mobilization factor, principal factor analysis of these indicators generated only a single factor with an eigenvalue greater than one. Table AP.3 on page 90 shows the loading of the indicators.

Table AP.3: Street Radicalism Component Factor Loading

Variable	Factor Loading
Election Acceptance	0.579966
Election Boycotts	0.650137
Anti-System Movements	0.347952
Sectarian Political Participation	0.05568

Control Variables

As described in Chapter 1, all statistical models in the monograph control for four prominent alternative explanations for democratization: modernization, regional diffusion, Western influence, and past level of democracy. This section details the specific source material and coding decisions for these control variables.

First, all tests control for the influence of modernization. Socio-economic modernization is the aspect of a country's politics that the largest number of scholars have argued affects that country's likelihood of democratizing (Lipset 1959, Teorell 2010). Modernization is a complex set of processes. However, at its core modernization is about a country's level of economic development, urbanization, and educational attainment. Thus, to control for modernization's influence on democracy, this monograph uses an aggregated modernization factor including measure of GDP per capita from the Maddisson Project, the infant mortality rate, the country's degree of urbanization, and the average number of years of education for children older than 15.[34]

- *GDP per Capita*: This variable is imported from V-Dem and transformed using the natural logarithm. The variable's original source is the Maddison Project. For details on their data collection process, see Bolt and van Zanden 2014 as well as the project's website: http://www.ggdc.net/maddison/maddison-project/home.htm.

- *Urbanization*: This variable is the ratio of the total urban population to the country's total population. Urban population is defined according to "the criteria of each area of country." This variable is imported from V-Dem. The original data come from the Clio-Infra project at the International Institute of Social History in the Netherlands. V-Dem then fills in missing years of data through linear interpolation. For more detail, see the V-Dem codebook, v7, pages 391-92 or the Clio-Infra project website at https://www.clio-infra.eu/.

Methodological Appendix

- *Education*: This variable is the average number of years of education received for those over the age of 15, with some years of missing data imputed using a linear model based on sources that measure the average years of educational attainment, primary school completion rate, secondary school enrollment rate, and literacy rate. This variable is imported from V-Dem. They base the variable on several original sources—primarily Clio Infra, but also data from the World Bank and others. For more detail, see the V-Dem codebook, v7, page 369 or the Clio Infra website at https://www.clio-infra.eu/.

- *Infant Mortality*: This base variable is the number of deaths prior to age 1 per 1000 live births in a year. This variable is then inverted so that the "good" outcome of lower infant mortality is at the high end of the variable, and thus the variable can be incorporated into a modernization factor. The variable is imported from V-Dem. They draw the data for the variable from Gapminder and Clio Infram and linearly interpolate missing data within a time series. For more detail, see the V-Dem codebook, v7, pages 389-390, and the Clio Infra and Gapminder websites at https://www.clio-infra.eu/ and www.gapminder.org respectively.

These four underlying indicators combine into a single factor with an eigenvalue above one, which is used as this study's indicator of modernization. The factor loading of the various underlying indicators is included in Table AP.4 below.

Table AP.4: Factor Loading for Modernization Factor

Variable	Factor Loading
GDP per capita (Logged)	0.804074
Urbanization	0.804613
Education	0.864839
Infant Mortality	0.847989

Many scholars have also argued that international factors are particularly important in explaining a country's level of democracy. There are two key types of international influence that are important to take into account: regional diffusion or a geographical proximity, that is to say the effect of being in a "democratic neighborhood" (Brinks and Coppedge 2006, Gleditsch and Ward 2006); and linkage with the West, that is to say the country's degree of social, economic, and political connection with the world's developed democracies (Levitsky and Way 2010, Ritter 2014). The monograph measures regional diffusion by measuring the percentage of democracies in each country's region.[35] The monograph also uses two measures of Western linkage. The first is the annual flow of exports and imports for each country to and from the United States, United Kingdom, Canada, Australia, and the Euro Area, as measured by the IMF, divided by GDP. The second is the country's degree of connectedness to the global network of International Non-Governmental Organizations (INGOs), as measured in the INGO Network Centrality Score (INCS) developed by Hughes and her co-authors (2009) and later expanded by Paxton and her co-authors (2015).

Finally, all statistical tests control for the level of democracy in the regime that preceded the civil resistance-led transition. This is measured by taking the average polyarchy score over the five years preceding the transition. Table AP.5 below contains summary statistics on all the variables included in the main statistical tests.

Table AP.5: Summary Statistics on Main Variables

Variable	N	Mean	Std. Dev	Min	Max
Mobilization	329	0.158	0.713	-1.804	1.725
Street Radicalism	329	0.077	0.704	-1.791	2.365
End of Transition Polyarchy	328	0.342	0.221	0.022	0.902
End of Transition Democracy	330	0.4	0.491	0	1
Old Regime Polyarchy	331	0.231	0.135	0.003	0.727
Modernization	331	-0.277	0.858	-2.389	1.829
INGO Linkage	328	0.208	0.196	0	0.836
Western Trade Linkage	331	0.028	0.105	0	1.5
Democratic Neighbors	331	0.204	0.196	0	1

Methodological Appendix

Detailed Statistical Results

The section below contains the detailed results for the four major statistical tests reported in the main text of the monograph: first, whether civil resistance at the beginning of a transition leads to higher levels of democracy; second, whether civil resistance at the beginning of a transition increases the likelihood of crossing the democratic threshold; third, whether within the population of civil resistance transitions, mobilization and street radicalism affect the level of democracy at the end of the transition; and fourth, whether they similarly affect the likelihood of crossing the democratic threshold. See Pinckney 2017 for robustness checks of these results using different operationalizations of the different concepts. All tests with the polyarchy score as the dependent variable are OLS models with robust standard errors clustered by country code. All tests with the binary measure of democracy from Geddes as the dependent variable are logistic regression models, also with country-clustered robust standard errors.

Table AP.6 contains the results of the OLS and logistic regression models described in Chapter 2 and depicted graphically in Figure 2.5 (Models 1 and 3), as well as OLS and logistic regression models of democratization that include only the structural factors and do not include the measure of whether a transition is a CRT (Models 2 and 4).

Table AP.6: Testing the Impact of CRTs on Post-Transition Democracy

	Model 1 OLS	Model 2 OLS	Model 3 Logistic	Model 4 Logistic
Civil Resistance Transition	.17082*** (.02386)		.17478*** (.35251)	
Modernization	.08080*** (.01486)	.09486*** (.01822)	.33418 (.19516)	.45256* (.19156)
Democratic Neighbors	.17754*** (.04580)	.19510*** (.05557)	2.1955** (.73813)	2.2438** (.78855)
Trade Linkage	-.00222 (.03674)	-.03200 (.04999)	-2.7575* (1.2291)	-2.4658* (1.2299)
INGO Network Centrality	.01669 (.05833)	.15342* (.06833)	.44740 (.91098)	1.6987* (.84765)
Previous Polyarchy Level	.47595*** (.08035)	.41672*** (.08564)	4.3594*** (1.1417)	3.3956** (1.0488)
Constant	.17431*** (.02980)	.20168*** (.03495)	-2.2646*** (.42905)	-1.8619*** (.40599)
N	325	325	328	328
r^2/Pseudo r^2	.54690	.46266	.23943	.17684

Robust standard errors, clustered by country, in parentheses
*$p < .05$, **$p < .01$, ***$p < 0.001$

Table AP.7 below contains the test results of the effects of the mobilization and street radicalism factors on the democracy level at the end of transition in CRTs. Figures 3.1 and 4.1 are both based on Model 5. Also included is a logistic regression model measuring the impact of these factors on the likelihood of exceeding the threshold level of democracy described above (Model 7), and Models of democratization in CRTs, including only the control variables and not considering the impact of mobilization and street radicalism (Models 6 and 8).

Table AP.7: Testing the Impact of Transitional Challenges on Post-Transition Democracy

	Model 5 OLS	Model 6 OLS	Model 7 Logistic	Model 8 Logistic
Mobilization	.14435*** (.02242)		1.3618* (.64450)	
Street Radicalism	-.11034*** (.02138)		-1.1566* (.47048)	
Modernization	.08702*** (.02206)	.16506*** (.02404)	-.36741 (.46251)	.40276 (.35299)
Trade Linkage	-.03504 (.13677)	.28123 (.18583)	2.6234 (2.3303)	2.2484 (1.8478)
Democratic Neighbors	.12801 (.08972)	.13194 (.11502)	5.9947 (13.950)	3.5794 (8.6007)
INGO Network Centrality	-.12019 (.08120)	-.08031 (.10362)	-1.3063 (1.4990)	-1.1631 (1.4689)
Previous Polyarchy Level	.10419 (.09765)	.15572 (.15376)	4.2910 (2.5792)	4.4670* (2.1413)
Constant	.38526*** (.04074)	.44059*** (.04991)	-.92897 (.97942)	-.09572 (.76290)
n	78	78	78	78
r^2/Pseudo r^2	.74790	.49902	.24894	.10385

Robust standard errors, clustered by country, in parentheses
*$p < .05$, **$p < .01$, ***$p < 0.001$

Table AP.8 on page 95 cross-tabulates the numbers of transitions, both CRTs and non-CRTs, that took place at varying levels of old regime democracy and whether these transitions ended in a democracy as coded by Geddes and her co-authors. These numbers inform Table 2.6.

Methodological Appendix

Table AP.8: Cross-Tabulation of Transitions and Old Regime Democracy

Civil Resistance Transition?	Post-Transition Democracy?	
	No	Yes
	Extremely Undemocratic	
No	101	28
Yes	9	26
	Mostly Undemocratic	
No	67	24
Yes	11	23
	Slightly Undemocratic	
No	9	20
Yes	0	7

Qualitative Research

As described in Chapter 1, qualitative research was conducted in three different countries: Zambia, Brazil and Nepal. These cases were selected following Lieberman's (2005) nested analysis research design. Lieberman argues that scholars who apply a single logic of inference to qualitative and quantitative methods of analysis such as King, Keohane and Verba (1994) are not appropriately leveraging the strengths of these distinct research methods. Instead of treating qualitative analysis as statistics with an insufficient number of cases, or quantitative analysis as comparative case study research with insufficient time to examine each case in depth, scholars should instead draw on what each of these approaches can offer to the other.

Lieberman suggests that scholars who wish to engage in this double-leveraging should use the following process: first, perform a large-n analysis to examine the robustness of one's theoretical model. If the model proves to be robust, the scholar then selects a certain number of cases that are well-predicted by the model for intensive case study analysis. The purpose of this analysis is to show that "the start, end, and intermediate steps of the model...explain the behavior of real world actors" (Lieberman 2005, 442). If the small-n analysis generally confirms the theorized mechanisms, then the scholar may conclude their analysis and make a convincing argument that their hypotheses have been supported. If either the large-n or small-n analysis fails to produce robust results, the scholar can return to an earlier step in the process, continuing to do so recursively until they either find satisfactory results or determine that their initial theoretical insight was flawed.

In addition to the criterion that cases in model-testing small-N analysis be well-predicted by the model, Lieberman also argues that scholars should select cases that show a wide degree of variation in the model's independent variables in order to demonstrate that the model's mechanisms operate in a wide number of different contexts, insofar as such variation can be incorporated with the general costs and benefits of conducting qualitative analysis (Lieberman 2005, 444). For this analysis, this meant selecting cases where mobilization and street radicalism varied.

A number of potential cases in the 78 CRTs fit these criteria. Three were selected based on widely different levels of mobilization and street radicalism, as well as widely divergent contextual conditions such as prior regime type, region, and time period.

For each case, interviews were conducted over roughly a month-long period of fieldwork. The fieldwork in Nepal took place from November 24, 2016 through December 23, 2016. The fieldwork in Zambia took place from March 17, 2017 through April 17, 2017. The fieldwork in Brazil took place from May 24, 2017 through June 30, 2017. In Nepal and Zambia, all interviews were conducted in person and in English by the author. In Brazil, the interviews were conducted in Brazilian Portuguese and then translated into English by Brazilian research assistants.

The total population of interviewees was drawn from across all relevant political and social cleavages so as to triangulate as complete as possible a picture of the transition dynamics. For instance, in Nepal, interviews were conducted with political leaders from all major parties: the Nepali Congress, the Communist Party of Nepal (United Marxist-Leninist) (CPN-UML), the Communist Party of Nepal (Maoist Center) CPN-MC, parties representing the Madhesi community from Southern Nepal, and members of the monarchical government under former King Gyanendra.

Interview subjects were identified through a combination of literature review, partnership with local informants, and advice from the initial population of interviewees. In each case, the author went through an extensive examination of media and scholarly sources on the political transition in question. During this examination, key decision-makers and participants in major transitional events were identified. Then, in preparation for the fieldwork, the author sought out publicly available contact information for these decision-makers and participants.

Once in the country, the author also supplemented this initial review process with substantive information from local partners. In Nepal, the research was conducted in partnership with the Nepal Peacebuilding Initiative, which provided the bulk of the names and contact information for interviewees. In Zambia, the research was conducted primarily in partnership with scholars of Zambian politics and history.. In Brazil, contacts through the University of Brasilia assisted the research.

Methodological Appendix

Prior to beginning the interview research, the study received approval from the University of Denver Institutional Review Board for the protection of human subjects. According to the terms of this approval, while subjects are identified as having participated in the study, their particular statements are kept de-identified to protect their confidentiality. Many of the events in question, particularly in Nepal, remain politically relevant and identifying some statements could lead to harm for particular subjects.

The interviews were semi-structured and roughly an hour in length, with some going as long as two hours and others as brief as 30 minutes. The interviews were structured following the advice of Leech (2002) and Berry (2002). The interviews themselves focused first on building rapport with the interviewees, asking them questions about their background and personal connection to the transitional events. After putting interviewees at ease, the remainder of the interview consisted largely of so-called grand tour questions in which the interviewee was invited to give an overview of what they considered to be the important events of the movement leading up to the transition and the transition itself. Grand tour questions would then typically be followed up with a set of fairly informal prompts, picking up on significant aspects of their answer to the grand tour question and asking them to elaborate. Direction by the interviewer was kept to a minimum, allowing the interviewee to offer whatever comments they thought relevant and appropriate.[36] The set of interview questions that shaped the semi-structured interviews is provided below:

The Pre-Transition Movement

- First, I'm going to ask you some questions about the events that led up to your country's political transition. I am interested in anything you can tell me about how [country-specific references to the movement that initiated the country's political transition – referred to hereafter as "the movement"] worked and how things that happened during the movement may have affected the political transition.
- Tell me about the movement. What were its major events?
    - o Follow-up: And what was your role and the role of your organization in this movement?
- How did the movement get started? And why did people choose to start it at that particular time?
- Was establishing democracy a key goal of the movement? What other goals were there?
- How did people in the movement deal with people from the old government who wanted to join? How welcome were they?
- What were the things that helped make the movement successful? What were the biggest challenges that it faced?
- How did people in the movement talk about the political transition? What challenges did you anticipate facing if you were successful in removing the old government from power?
- What kind of plans did people in the movement make for the political transition? Did people in the movement plan to continue protests and other activism during the political transition?

- Would you say that the movement succeeded in achieving its goals?

Transitional Challenges

- Now I'm going to ask you some questions about the political transition after the old government was removed. I am interested in understanding what challenges there were in moving your country toward democracy and how you and other people from the movement tried to address these challenges.
- Tell me about the transition. What were the major events? How did things change and how did they stay the same?
- What aspects of your country's politics made establishing democracy easier? What things made it harder?
- Specifically, how did your role and your organization's role change?
    - o Follow-up if necessary: For example, did you enter politics? Did you try to pursue different kinds of policies? Did you organize new protests or strikes?
    - o Follow-up: Why did you and your organization pursue this path? What did you want to accomplish?
- Did other people from the movement or other political groups still organize protests, strikes, or other kinds of extreme political action?
    - o Follow-up if yes: Who organized these kinds of actions?
    - o Follow-up if yes: What kinds of tactics did they use?
    - o Follow-up if yes: What kinds of goals did they pursue?
    - o Follow-up if yes: What was the reaction to this kind of action from people who were now in power?
- Were people from the old government punished in any way for abuses they had committed while in power? Why or why not?
    - o Follow-up if yes: What kind of punishment was there? Who did it apply to and how heavy were the penalties?
    - o Follow-up if yes: How did the people from the old government facing punishment react? Did they try to prevent the punishment in any way?
- How much agreement or disagreement was there between groups within the old movement about what the new political system should look like? Were disagreements resolved, and if so how?
- What were the most important political divisions during the transition?
    - o Follow-up: For example, divisions over ethnicity, religion, economic class, or political ideology.
- Who got to participate in making political decisions during the transition? Who was left out?
    - o Follow-up: How did people who were left out respond? How did they try and get

Methodological Appendix

people to listen to their agenda?
- How did the new people in power deal with members of the old government? Who was allowed to stay in politics? Who was not allowed to stay in politics?
    - Follow-up: If people from the old government could participate in politics, what was their role? How central were they in the new government?
- How democratic would you say your country is today? Completely democratic, mostly democratic, a little democratic, or not democratic at all.
    - Follow-up (if not fully democratic): What is keeping your country from being fully democratic?
    - Follow-up (if fully democratic): What are the things that support your country's democratic system?
- What else should I know about your country that we haven't talked about yet?

Endnotes

[1] See also the International Center on Nonviolent Conflict's forthcoming Key Terms in the Study and Translation of Civil Resistance: https://www.nonviolent-conflict.org/key-terms-study-translation-civil-resistance/.

[2] The specific statistical techniques used by Celestino and Gleditsch make it difficult to put an exact number on this likelihood. See pages 394-396 of their article for a discussion of this difficulty.

[3] For more details on the specific mechanisms whereby nonviolent resistance helps civil society during political transitions, see Bayer, Bethke, and Dressler 2017.

[4] Survival analysis is a statistical modeling technique developed to measure the impact of medical interventions on patient survival. Thus, it is ideally suited for answering questions about how particular factors will affect the "lifespan" of other types of things, such as democratic political regimes.

[5] For details on how these different dimensions are averaged together, and the underlying indicators that make up the indexes, see the Varieties of Democracy codebook at https://www.v-dem.net/en/data/data-version-7/. See also the more extensive discussion of these variables in Pinckney 2017.

[6] Since this is meant to measure an ideal type, no country ever receives a 1, or a 0. Scores range from 0.009 to 0.949.

[7] For more detail on this definition, see Geddes, Wright and Frantz 2014b, pp 7-8.

[8] See the methodological appendix for details on how these control variables are measured as well as summary statistics on all these variables.

[9] Due to political unrest in Brazil during the research period, as well as the greater length of time that had passed between the events in question and the interviews, the number of interviews conducted in Brazil was significantly smaller than in Nepal and Zambia. Thus, the examples and information from Brazil rely to a greater extent on the already existing scholarly literature.

[10] More information on the fieldwork, including the dates and interview questionnaire is included in the methodological appendix.

[11] The vertical axes in these graphs report the absolute numbers of transitions that ended with polyarchy scores in the range reported on the horizontal axes. For instance, the first column in the right-hand graph (CRTs) shows that six civil resistance transitions ended with polyarchy scores between 0.1 and 0.2. The numbers are higher on the left-hand graph (Non-CRTs) because there are more transitions not initiated by nonviolent resistance overall.

[12] As described in the previous chapter, these measurements are taken at the point after the breakdown of a political regime where the level of fluctuation in the polyarchy score declines to a minimal level. In other words, the measurement is taken at the point at which the country has settled into a level of democracy that it will continue in for a lengthy period into the future.

[13] The difference between CRTs and Non-CRTs is similar if one reduces the threshold level of democracy to a polyarchy score of 0.5 (56% of CRTs are above this threshold, compared to 16% of non-CRTs) or even

a low threshold of a polyarchy score of 0.4 (67% of CRTs are above this threshold compared to 28% of non-CRTs).

[14] The statistical tests reported are an OLS model and a logistic regression model. See the methodological appendix for more details.

[15] The vertical lines extending from each of the four points are 95% confidence intervals, meaning that for each point we can be 95% sure that the actual level of democracy or probability of democracy falls somewhere in that range.

[16] To be precise, the marginal effect of moving from a 0 to 1 on the CRT measure is roughly equivalent to a marginal effect of moving from 0 to 0.44 on the measure of pre-transition average polyarchy score.

[17] Extremely undemocratic countries had a pre-transition polyarchy score below 0.2. Moderately undemocratic countries had a pre-transition polyarchy score between 0.2 and 0.4. Only slightly undemocratic countries had a polyarchy score between 0.4 and 0.6.

[18] See methodological appendix table AP.7 for a cross-tabulation of the absolute numbers for these categories.

[19] Mobilization was measured by combining counts of protests and strikes with measures of the degree of public deliberation and civil society activity. For details on the methodology used to construct this measurement, see the methodological appendix and also Pinckney 2017. The statistical model also controls for the influence of contextual factors as in the models of the impact of nonviolent resistance described in Chapter 2.

[20] The central solid line in the figure shows the predicted level of democracy at the end of a civil resistance-initiated political transition across the spectrum of possible levels of mobilization. The dashed lines show the upper and lower bounds of a 95% confidence interval, meaning we can be 95% sure that the actual value falls within that range.

[21] A difference of 0.35 is roughly equivalent to the difference between Sweden's level of democracy and Lebanon's level of democracy in 2016.

[22] The labels on the x axis of this graph are intended to facilitate interpretation. The mobilization variable is continuous, rather than categorical, and thus there are no sharp divisions between transitions with, for example, very low and low levels of mobilization. See the methodological appendix for more detail.

[23] For instance, in Ukraine and Russia such organizations are sometimes derogatorily referred to as Grantoyedy, or "grant eaters" (Squier 2002, 181).

[24] There is an extensive literature on these dynamics across many different countries and international NGOs. For examples, see Carpenter 2007, Cooley and Ron 2002, Koch et al 2009, Morfit 2011, and Schuller 2012.

[25] "Dalit" is a term used to refer to that class of people in the Hindu caste system historically referred to as "untouchables." Dalits are traditionally considered to be at the bottom of the caste system, and face significant discrimination in social, political, and economic arenas across South Asia.

[26] See the methodological appendix for more detail on the interviewees for this project.

[27] This model of radicalization of politics follows a similar logic to Rabushka and Shepsle's (1972) analysis

of politics in "plural" societies but expands the scope beyond ethnic or cultural divisions.

[28] This monograph's measure of street radicalism involves statistically combining measures of the degree of activity by "anti-system movements," the presence of electoral boycotts, the acceptance of electoral results, and whether a country's political competition is "sectarian." For more detail on all these measures and the statistical methods used to combine them, see the methodological appendix included in this monograph and Pinckney 2017.

[29] The solid line at the center is the predicted level of post-transition democracy, while the dashed lines above and below it are a 95% confidence interval, meaning that we can be 95% sure that a country with this level of street radicalism will have a level of democracy within the range of the two dashed lines. The labels on the x axis of this graph are intended to facilitate interpretation. The street radicalism variable is continuous, rather than categorical, and thus there are no sharp divisions between transitions with, for example, very low and low levels of mobilization. See the methodological appendix for more detail.

[30] Nepal's former king has remained in Nepal and often expressed a desire to return to power because of the disruptive and destructive nature of Nepal's politics since his ouster. See the Kathmandu Post, October 21, 2017. "Ex-King Gyanendra says time has come for his leadership." http://kathmandupost.ekantipur.com/news/2017-10-21/ex-king-gyanedra-says-time-has-come-for-his-leadership.html.

[31] One analysis estimates that general strikes from 2008 to 2013 led to economic losses of over 100 billion dollars, increased inflation, and significantly depressed Nepal's GDP growth rate (Shrestha and Chaudhary 2014).

[32] NAVCO 2.1 is a revised and expanded version of the NAVCO 2.0 dataset initially produced by Chenoweth and Lewis (2013).

[33] The Geddes data only goes through 2010. I personally coded the data forward through 2015 to capture any additional regime breakdowns. I detail this process and provide justification for any additional regime breakdown codings in Pinckney 2017.

[34] These measures are combined using principal factor analysis, a statistical technique that uses the variance-covariance matrix of different variables to determine whether the pattern of particular variables can be explained by a single underlying (but unobservable) dimension. Factor analysis of the four modernization measures yields only a single factor with an eigenvalue above one, strongly indicating that there is only a single dimension underlying these measures, which is retained as the measure of modernization. For more detail on the use of factor analysis in political science research, see Teorell 2010 or Hendrix 2010.

[35] The data on percentage of democracies in a region comes from Haber and Menaldo (2011).

[36] Some additional sources that informed the interview research methodology were McCracken (1988) and Spradley (1979).

Acknowledgements

This project has benefited from more people than I can possibly name. First, I am deeply grateful for the careful supervision and mentorship of my PhD dissertation advisor Erica Chenoweth and the members of my dissertation committee: Cullen Hendrix, Aaron Schneider, and Tim Sisk.

I would like to thank my interviewees in all three countries. In Nepal, my thanks go to Subindra Bogati, Ches Thurber and Chiranjibi Bhandari for helping identify interview contacts. In Zambia, the same thanks goes to Miles Larmer, Adrienne LeBas, Nic Cheeseman, Marja Hinfelaar, Sishuwa Sishuwa, and Akashambatwa Mbikusita-Lewanika. In Brazil, thanks to my research assistants: Karine Fernandes, Fabricio Freitas, Paula Moreira, and Isabela Ottoni, and to Fernando Horta, who hosted me in Brasilia.

My thanks also goes to all those who have offered comments on early versions of the research, particularly Luke Abbs, Consuelo Amat, Colin Beck, Felix Bethke, Charles Butcher, Killian Clarke, John Chin, Kristian Skrede Gleditsch, Milli Lake, George Lawson, Liesel Mitchell, Benjamin Naimark-Rowse, Sharon Nepstad, Daniel Ritter, Ches Thurber, and one anonymous reviewer.

During the time spent on this project I had the joy of being part of two communities of incredible scholars, first in the PhD program at the Josef Korbel School of International Studies and then in the Institute of Sociology and Political Science at NTNU. Every one of my colleagues has been kind, supportive, and encouraging. I would like to particularly thank Joel Day, Kyleanne Hunter, Pauline Moore, and Chris Shay.

I am grateful to the International Center on Nonviolent Conflict for supporting this research and bringing this monograph about. In particular I would like to thank Maciej Bartkowski, Amber French, and Hardy Merriman.

Finally, my love and gratitude goes out to my family and friends – particularly my parents Coty and Beth Pinckney and Kandyce Pinckney – for their patience, love, and support.

www.ingramcontent.com/pod-product-compliance
Lightning Source LLC
Chambersburg PA
CBHW041646040426

R18086900002B/R180869PG42333CBX00018B/11